MEDITERRANEAN SAILING

Rod Heikell

NAUTICAL

First published in Great Britain by Nautical Books
an imprint of A&C Black (Publishers) Ltd
35 Bedford Row, London, WC1R 4JH

ISBN 0 7136 5850 9

By the same author
Greek Waters Pilot
Italian Waters Pilot
Mediterranean Cruising Handbook
Turkish Waters Pilot

Filmset by August Filmsetting, Haydock, St Helens
Printed in Great Britain by Butler & Tanner Ltd,
Frome and London

...kas Island in Greece. The effect of a ...d mass on wind direction and strength.

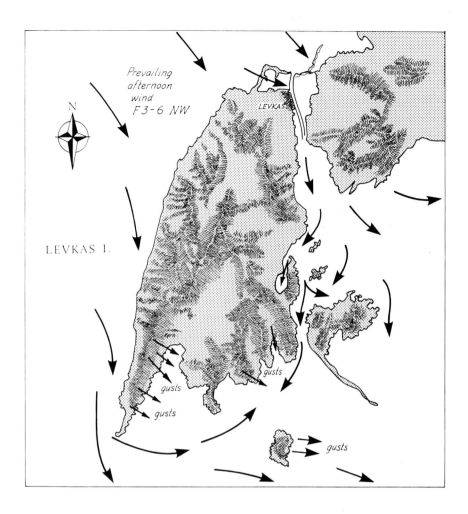

Acknowledgement

Many people helped get together the information for this book and although I can't name them all, I hope I include most of them here. My thanks to Jim Baesalman for looking over the chapters on anchoring and berthing, to Gilly Baesalman for helpful comments on the chapter on health, to Pru Farrington for helpful comments on anchoring and berthing, to Neville Bulphit and Graham Sewell for looking over the chapter on navigation and pilotage, to Helen Penney for some useful comments on several of the chapters, to Colin Michel for sorting out problems and Yvette for long distance calls, to Peter Johnson for setting it all in motion, and to Joe Charlton and Robyn, Mark Welch, Nessy Jones, Yener of Seagull Sailmakers, Ahmet of Bitez, Nigel Wadlow and Dot Wilson. Thanks also to Nautical Books' editor Peter Coles for putting the whole act together.

I am also grateful to Falcon Sailing and the Yacht Cruising Association for photographs.

3

Contents

Preface   6

1   The Mediterranean   9

2   Weather Matters   21

3   Harbours   39

4   Anchoring   55

5   Navigation and Pilotage   70

6   Staying Healthy   85

7   Marine Life   97

8   Mediterranean Pot-pourri   115

Appendix   140

Index   142

Preface

On a map of the world the Mediterranean looks like a big lake at the bottom of Europe. Compared to the Atlantic, it looks like a backwater creek running inland from the sea. But it exerts a pull way beyond its geographical scale on all of us. For some, it is a place where the sun shines from an azure sky, over an anchorage with a few white fishermen's houses ashore. For others, the virtual absence of tides removes at a stroke a complication of sailing that has bedevilled them for years. It is warm spray over the bows, from a blue sea. It is a sea stretching from the Occident to the Orient, a sea surrounded by a variety of countries and cultures that have played a significant part in shaping our own history. For the archaeology enthusiast it is a goldmine. Whatever the images are, they exercise a powerful pull on us to visit this sea and sail around it: although you'll have to find out for yourself whether they reflect the reality. What this book is designed to do is to help you get your boat safely and enjoyably around the Mediterranean, whether you are there for a year or two or a fortnight.

There are problems particular to the Mediterranean, and variations on problems encountered in sailing elsewhere. The weather for instance. In many parts of the world weather patterns can be reliably predicted by observing cloud, pressure and wind changes, and weather stations can give you a forecast with reasonable accuracy by analysing these and using satellite data. In the Mediterranean the track and speed of a depression can vary so much that weather forecasts give little indication of what is going to happen locally, or worse give you yesterday's weather. Thermal effects in the summer can change the weather with frightening rapidity from a flat calm to a gale in half an hour. There are also new techniques to learn and old ones to be refined. Berthing Mediterranean style, either stern or bows-to the quay with an anchor holding you off, is the accepted practice in nine out of ten harbours, and you are going to have to learn to do it without fuss or bother — even when the space looks impossibly small and it's blowing half a gale. Anchoring techniques need to be carefully examined as you will often be anchoring in deep water on a weedy bottom that will apparently defy your best attempts at getting the anchor to bite.

Navigation and pilotage might appear to be universal skills wherever you are, but in different parts of the world special problems crop up and the Mediterranean is no exception. Piloting by eye must be honed to a fine art if you are going to get safely around the coast and into strange harbours and anchorages: no amount of electronic wizardry can replace your eyes and that wonderfully compact computer under the cranium. Many of the charts you will be using were surveyed in the 19th century and despite the best endeavours of hydrography departments to keep them up-to-date and accurate, they are not always so.

As well as the technical topics covered here, there is information on health in a hot climate, marine life, the geography and history of the Mediterranean region: the sort of information the thinking yachtsman will want to know about. In the last chapter I have assembled a diverse mixture of subjects that quite simply didn't fit anywhere else. Much of it, such as food, wine, flora, archaeological sites and guidebooks, has nothing specifically to do with sailing but is important to many of us however we travel. Other sections on official paperwork and chartering are more obviously linked to sailing. In the chapters covering weather, anchoring, berthing, navigation and the like, I may be accused of attempting to cover too much in too little space. What I have set out to do is cover the aspects of these subjects that are pertinent to sailing in the Mediterranean and not to write a general treatise on each of them. Inevitably there is some overlap of more general information on these subjects, and where there are obvious gaps you will need to turn to other books.

This whole collection of information, from weather and anchoring to food and wine, is linked by its common relationship to the Mediterranean. I have been accused of having a passion for this giant inland sea, and it is true. Inevitably the images I have of it have changed over time: the shores around the sea are changing. Monstrous holiday villages have been built in once deserted bays. Small fishing villages have succumbed to a pernicious tourism that submerges the old village values to the new values of the currency exchange rate. But it is nonsense to say that the Med has been ruined. If you go to Benidorm, Nice, San Remo or Mykonos then you deserve the opinions you will come away with. Yet within a day's sail of any of these are idyllic anchorages and small fishing harbours. Last year I sat in Spetsai in Greece waiting for my crew to turn up. It was August and the outer harbour was jammed full of boats. When the crew arrived we departed straight away and went to a harbour eleven miles away. In Leonidhion all was peace and quiet with only a few other yachts to keep us company.

Some people can travel, whether on land or water, and never see what is all around them. There seems little point in sailing in the Mediterranean if you are not aware of what is there. A long time ago Plotinus said, 'To any vision must be brought an eye adapted to what is to be seen'. This book is intended to solve the problems of sailing so that you can enjoy seeing where you are. Take your time and enjoy being there.

1
The Mediterranean

In the Atlantic and Pacific Oceans the thing that stands out is the large tracts of water between the land and islands. The trade wind belt, the doldrums and the Sargasso Sea, breeding grounds for hurricanes, the Humboldt current and the Gulf Stream, the roaring forties: the interaction of wind and water defines these oceans and much of the character of the bordering lands. To make sense of the Mediterranean you have to turn this feature inside out and look at the land as defining the sea, the largest and most important inland sea in the world although small in size and volume compared to the oceans. To those who cruise on the waters of the Mediterranean, it is this feature, the land which surrounds the sea and the islands dotted about it, which gives the sea its appeal.

Profile of an inland sea

Geography

At its longest the Mediterranean is 3700 kilometres (2300 miles), from Gibraltar to Iskenderun; and at its widest with a bit of a dog-leg, it is 1800 kilometres (1100 miles) from Trieste at the top of the Adriatic to the Gulf of Sirte in Libya. The surface area is 2.96 million square kilometres (1.46 million square miles). Of importance to the yachtsman is its long coastline, enormously increased by the long peninsulas like Italy, the much indented coastlines of countries like Greece and Turkey, and the myriad islands. Apart from the well known larger islands like Majorca, Corsica, Sardinia, Sicily, Evia, Crete and Cyprus, there are thousands of others of all shapes and sizes down to small uninhabited rocks. The complex outline of the mainland and the islands makes it virtually impossible to calculate a figure for the total length of coastline, but some idea of just how large this would be can be gained from the fact that Sardinia's is over 1100 miles and Sicily's over 1400 miles.

The Mediterranean is not only small but comparatively shallow in comparison to the oceans. Its area is about 1/140th of the total sea area of the world, but its volume is a mere 1/355th. The mean depth is 1500 metres and even its greatest depth, at 4600 metres southwest of Cape Matapan in Greece, is only slightly more than the mean depth of the Atlantic. There is a paradox here because although the Mediterranean is not deep in oceanographic terms, to yachtsmen it is. There is very little water shallower than 50 metres right up to the coast in most places, so that one of the delights is being able to sail close to the shore and sightsee without running aground. The virtual absence of tides means that the depth changes little.

a.

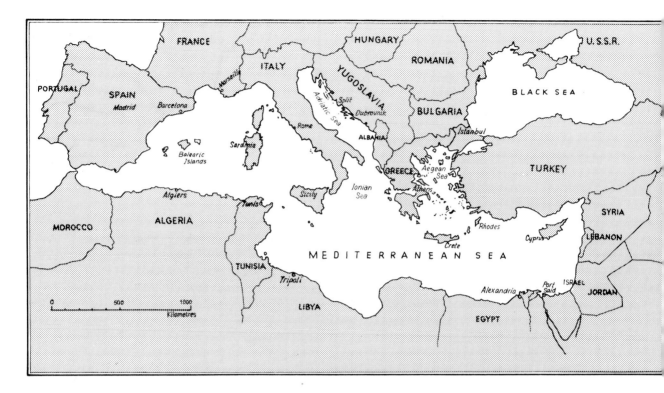

The Mediterranean.

If we look at the Mediterranean in cross-section, a feature that stands out is the ridges separating the basins. The principal ridge at Gibraltar, between the Atlantic and the western Mediterranean, is 320 metres down; that between Sicily and Tunisia 400 metres, and in the Bosphorus the sill is only 40 metres deep. These features are important not just geologically but for the character of the sea as well. The shallow ridge between the Atlantic and the western basin shuts out the effect of the Atlantic tides, and as the volume of water in the Mediterranean is comparatively so small, the gravitational pull of the sun and the moon does not generate any great tidal range there. Salinity in the eastern basin is higher than in the western basin where Atlantic water decreases the salt content. The ridges containing the western and eastern basins tend to confine some marine life to these areas, especially the smaller species, so that a large number of Mediterranean species are not found elsewhere, or at least not in great numbers.

The hydrology of this almost totally enclosed sea is complex. Evaporation from the surface causes an annual loss of around 2900 cubic kilometres of water, about 1/1000 of the total volume. Only about half of this is replaced by rainfall on the sea or the catchment areas draining into it, so there is an annual imbalance of around 1450 cubic kilometres of water, around 100,000 gallons a second for every second in a year. You don't need any great mathematical ability to see that a lot of water has to come from somewhere, and it is made up from the Atlantic pouring in through the Straits of Gibraltar. This means a constant east-going stream of some $2\frac{1}{2}$ knots, which increases up to 6 knots when the Atlantic tides help it along, making this the only place in the Mediterranean where you really have to study the tide-tables and wait for the tide in your favour if you are sailing west. The water pouring in over the Gibraltar sill also causes the predominantly anti-clockwise circulation of surface water around the two basins. From Gibraltar a current travels along the North African coast to the Sicilian Channel where some of it is forced up inside Italy to circulate around the western basin. The rest flows on along the North African coast until it is in turn forced up around the Aegean. These surface currents are not appreciable, except where the water is forced through a narrow channel or around headlands, for instance in the Strait of Messina between Italy and Sicily or in the narrow channel between Evia and mainland Greece. In most other places a constant wind oppos-ing the flow will reverse its direction.

While water flows in from the Atlantic, there is a substantial flow out as well. The water of the Mediterranean is more saline than the water of the oceans, about 39 parts of salt per 1000 of water compared to 35 parts per 1000 for the Atlantic, and this denser water sinks and flows slowly westwards to spill over the sill at Gibraltar into the Atlantic; it can be detected as far out as the Azores and the Bay of Biscay. It takes around 180 years for the total volume of water in the Mediterranean to be renewed, and if there were not this outflow it would become ever saltier until it was transformed into a dead sea unable to support life, a situation that existed when it was a totally enclosed basin some six million years ago in the Messinian period.

Geology

Seventy million years ago the Mediterranean did not exist. Between the continents the great Tethys Ocean stretched from the Indo—West Pacific region clear across between the African and European continents to the Americas. Over millions of years the Arabian continent pushed up towards Turkey on the Eurasian plate, forming and eventually closing the eastern end of the Mediterranean. Some 40 million years ago the African plate which had pushed right up to Europe began to move away, until about nine million years ago the Mediterranean looked pretty much as we see it today.

One further cataclysmic event was to take place. Around six million years ago the Mediterranean was shut off from the Atlantic by a land bridge between Morocco and Gibraltar. The salts from the evaporated sea accumulated to a depth of two kilometres in places and it is still down there on the sea floor. The Mediterranean would have looked much like a salt desert with saline lakes and quicksands; and around the rivers green oases would have grown on the silt brought down. Perhaps early man or his forebears hunted in these oases. For half a million years the Mediterranean basin remained like this until the Atlantic burst through the western end and turned it back into a sea. However it hap-pened, a giant waterfall over the top of the sill or an earth tremor destroying part of the barrier, it would have been spectacular. It has been said that this is what got prehistoric man up onto two feet – so he could run away to safety.

By the time man had arrived on the scene, the Mediterranean would have looked much like it does now. Some anthropologists have hypothesized land bridges across the Mediterranean in the various Ice Ages of the Pleistocene period, but calculation shows this to have been unlikely. The two shallowest parts of the sea are now the ridges between Sicily and North Africa at 400 metres and between Gibraltar and Morocco at 320 metres. When the world's water was locked up in the glacial sheets of an Ice Age it is estimated that the surface level of the oceans and seas dropped by as much as 100 metres, not nearly enough to expose the sea floor over these ridges. So man probably took the

Greek caiques and Baroque architecture. The hull form reflects the Orient, the architecture the Occiden

long route around the Levant to reach Europe from Africa, unless he could somehow float across the gap between Morocco and Gibraltar.

The forces that sculpted the Mediterranean, the giant tectonic plates of the various land masses, are still on the move today. Where they meet, the earth is folded and buckled into the fractured mountain ranges so evident throughout the Mediterranean. The floor under and around the sea lies on a gigantic geological jigsaw puzzle of plates: the Iberian pushes on the African and Apulian plates, the Apulian pushes on the Iberian and Eurasian plates, the Eurasian plate pushes on the Apulian and African plates and at one point touches the Iberian plate, and the African plate pushes in turn on the Eurasian and Iberian plates. Occasionally one of them will give a little shunt to settle itself and when this happens the result can be catastrophic. On November 23, 1980 Italy was nudged gently towards Yugoslavia. For a few minutes the earth rocked and groaned and when the dust cleared part of Italy had been flattened. Over 5000 people were killed and nearly half a million left homeless. Seventeen southern towns were totally demolished and many other towns and villages suffered major damage. The junctions of the earth's plates are often marked on the surface by volcanoes, and this is nowhere more evident than along the west coast of Italy. From Etna on Sicily the chain continues on through the Aeolian Islands, with Vulcano and Stromboli still active, to Vesuvius and the Phlegraean Fields near Naples. Vesuvius has been quiet since 1944 but the earth around Pozzuoli in the Phlegraean Fields has been rising recently, indicating that magma is again accumulating under the surface. If this volcano erupted it is estimated that Naples could be buried under a hundred metres of ash, but it may not happen for another thousand years or so.

In other parts of the Mediterranean the effects of the magma beneath the surface are more benignly demonstrated. In most of the countries you can find natural hot springs in often idyllic locations. As the warm water works its way to the surface it absorbs salts, and in some areas picks up a little radioactivity as well, to become a watery cocktail celebrated in the world famous spas dotted around the Mediterranean. Many are not well known and one of my favourites is in Turkey in a deserted bay where a rock pool about the size of a bath is at just the right temperature, with a view over the bay and islands behind. Some hedonistic god got it just right.

Historical Perspectives

The geographical and geological picture is a partial view of the Mediterranean that the thinking visitor will want to fill in with the peoples and cultures around it. Such a description and history would be difficult to fit into a large book without skimping here and there. Those interested in the labyrinth of civilizations and peoples that have populated the Mediterranean from prehistory to the present, will find in the appendix at the back a list of useful books. What I can do here is paint a broad canvas with the Mediterranean in the centre of it. This thin gash between the continents has historically separated completely different worlds and it still does. The divisions may be blurred by the political boundaries defining the eighteen countries now surrounding the Mediterranean, but the overall picture is there and it takes something like the fundamentalist Islamic revolution in Iran which has spread to the Levant, or the partitioning of Cyprus in 1974, to bring these wider divisions to the surface.

The Mediterranean straddles the Occident and the Orient; taking Italy as a dividing line, everything to the west is the Occident and to the east the Orient. This is made immediately obvious in the cuisine of the two regions. In the west thick soups, oven-baked dishes and rich sauces predominate, whereas in the east cold starters, spicy grilled kebabs and meatballs, and simple salads are the mainstay of the diet. In the 19th and early 20th centuries the division was still an accepted one referred to in travel books of the era. In *Eothen*, which means 'from the east', A.W. Kinglake describes his journey through Greece, Turkey, Cyprus and the Levant in the 1830s as an 'Oriental tour'. Most other travel writers of the period similarly described 'the Orient'. After the Second World War the division between Occident and Orient was used less, as parts of the Orient apparently became Occidental, but anyone who visits the countries in the eastern Mediterranean soon understands that under the western surface an Oriental heart still beats.

From this broad division between west and east, it is useful to reconsider the Mediterranean as a whole and this time carve it into 'three huge, thriving civilizations, three major modes of thinking, believing, eating, drinking and living' (Braudel). These divisions exist intact not only in the present, but can be traced through the convoluted history of the Mediterranean from very early on. And from this inland sea the impact of the three civilizations stretches thousands of miles, across the oceans on either side and to the continents to the north and south.

The first of these is the western culture corresponding to the Occident. It is the Christian world, formerly the Roman Catholic world, with Rome at the hub. As such it spread north to split into the Protestant church and its myriad offspring, and from there Catholic and Protestant together migrated to the New World and colonised it. So much of our current mythology – the Protestant ethic, the idea of progress as a good and worthy object, of converting those in far away lands to our western ideals – evolved from the old Latin universe centred in Rome. In Europe it can be difficult to see this, but in America the religious underpinning of western ideals is more obvious.

The second division is the Greek Orthodox world. Until quite recently western historians paid only scant attention to Byzantium and its legacy, indeed few of us comprehend the extent today of the Orthodox Church and fewer still its antecedents. From Greece the Orthodox Church covers the Balkan peninsula, Bulgaria, part of Yugoslavia, Romania and north up to the vastness of Russia. The barrier of the Eastern Bloc disguises its extent, but any traveller to the region will tell you that it is alive even if not highly visible. Until the Ottoman Turks over-ran it in 1453, the Orthodox Church, then the Holy Roman Empire in the east, the Byzantine Empire, had its centre at Constantinople. Since then Orthodoxy has been without a centre although not without power. The central figure in the Cyprus troubles in the 1960s was Makarios, the somewhat sinister Greek Orthodox Archbishop, who in effect wanted Cyprus to be wholly part of the Greek Orthodox world. However, Islam and the Turkish Army eventually decided otherwise.

Islam is the third slice of the Mediterranean, starting at Turkey on the eastern end of the Mediterranean and running around its southern shores to Morocco. It extends from there into Africa, across the Indian Ocean to Indonesia, the Philippines and the islands in the Melanesian archipelago. Islam has recently asserted itself with the new fundamentalism centred on Iran, spreading from there to Lebanon and fomenting the bloody civil war between Muslim and Christian, and appearing farther east. The effect of Islam on the Mediterranean was considerable when the Ottoman Empire held sway over all of Greece, the Balkans, and threatened Italy and Malta. From North Africa the Arab invasions of Spain introduced Islam at the western end of the Mediterranean. The legacy of Islam was not just the obvious cultural influences as seen in cuisine, music and dress, but also on agriculture with the introduction of new species and methods of irrigation, in science and in architecture, influences which spread throughout the Catholic and Orthodox worlds and remained after the Turks and Arabs left. One of our most popular beverages, coffee,

*tilini on Lesvos. A little bit of Italy
splanted into the Levant.*

was one of Islam's legacies to the west.

From these three divisions further sub-divisions can be made. Some are a part of one of the major civilizations, others combine parts of them. The Levant brings together the Orthodox islands close to Asia Minor and stretches down this coast to include Syria, Lebanon and across to Cyprus. The Mahgreb pulls together Tunisia, Algeria and Morocco, reflecting their interlocked history and cultural roots. The Balkans include northern Greece, Bulgaria, Romania and Yugoslavia as an area with much history and culture in common. In the Occidental half of the Mediterranean it is more difficult today to pick out the larger patterns that once shaped the history of these countries.

The pegs I have arranged, on which to hang the multi-coloured coats of the Mediterranean countries, are there to make a broad sense of the layers of accumulated history and intermingled cultures that at first sight appears as a tangle, seemingly impossible to penetrate. Sometimes the political boundary of a country conceals a great deal more than it reveals. After all, no other region has experienced such a concentrated and lengthy period of building up civilizations and demolishing others; from the very first hunters and gatherers in the Mesopotamian valley through the Egyptians, Hittites, Assyrians, Minoans and Myceneans, Greeks, Romans, Arabs, Byzantium, Franks, Ottomans, Venetians and Genoese, the Papal States, the Spanish, French, British and Russians, to the First and Second World Wars and the division of the Mediterranean into the 18 countries around its shores today. Try to recite that list quickly!

15

Cruising areas

We all have preconceptions about what to expect when we travel and one of the marvellous things is that these preconceptions are so often shattered. I do not want to do this before you arrive and it is unlikely that I could, but if you are going cruising or chartering a boat it is useful to have an outline of what a country is like and what to expect of the area. The following is a brief roundup of some salient facts for the countries around the Mediterranean.

Gibraltar This tiny country, just over 2 square miles in area, is a base rather than a cruising area. There are two marinas and all facilities for yachts. 'The Rock', as it is affectionately called, is in some respects more English than England, and you either love it or hate it. From Gibraltar you can cruise to the Atlantic coast of Spain and Portugal, to the Mediterranean coast of Spain and across to Morocco.

Spain The Mediterranean coast of Spain stretches for some 750 miles from Gibraltar to the French border. There are a number of large wide gulfs, but on the whole it is not deeply indented. It is divided into five 'costas' which broadly reflect the characteristics of each section of coast. The Costa del Sol, the sunny coast, extends from Gibraltar for 155 miles; the Costa Blanca or white coast, for the next 200 miles to Cabo de San Antonio; the Costa del Azahar, known as the orange blossom coast, for 115 miles to Cabo Tortosa; the Costa Dorada or golden coast, for 140 miles to Rio Tordera; and the Costa Brava for the last 67 miles to the French border. There is one large group of offshore islands, the Balearics, composed of Ibiza, Majorca, and Menorca, lying 50 miles off mainland Spain.

The Spanish coast and the Balearics have long been popular for cruising and considerable numbers of boats are kept there permanently. Numerous new marinas have been built to accommodate these boats and visitors, but despite the numbers of boats and additional tourists there are still many attractive anchorages and fishing harbours away from the crowds. Ashore there are good facilities for yachts at the marinas, but in out-of-the-way places these are less evident. Eating out varies from good and basic, to terrible and basic imitations of the worst of English food in the popular tourist areas, but on the whole real Spanish cuisine is excellent.

France The coast stretches for 330 miles from the Spanish border and the Pyrenees to the Italian border and the Alps. It can be divided into four areas. Languedoc-Rousillon, a low marshy area and part of the Rhone river delta, has recently been extensively developed with large marina complexes. The Cote Bleue, the blue coast, extends from the Rhone to Cap Sicie. The Cote d'Azur, the azure coast, extends from Cap Sicie to Cap Ferrat and includes fashionable St Tropez and Cannes. The French Riviera, arguably the oldest tourist region in the Mediterranean, includes the principality of Monaco and abuts the Italian Riviera. The large island of Corsica a hundred miles offshore adds an additional 350 miles of spectacular coastline to the French total.

The coast of France has long been the mecca of Mediterranean yachting and there are probably more marinas per mile than anywhere else in the world. Also, many of the fishing harbours have been converted to accommodate yachts. There are few sheltered anchorages so most cruising must perforce be from one marina to another. There are excellent facilities for yachts, and since people have been coming here for holidays since the 19th century there is everything and anything Gallic ashore, including some of the finest cuisine in the Mediterranean.

Corsica offers superb cruising under majestic mountain scenery. Again, many of the fishing harbours have acquired marinas and ashore facilities are well developed. A word

Au natur

of warning: the Corsicans do not consider themselves French even if things ashore do not seem all that different from the mainland.

Italy This long peninsula juts 500 miles into the Mediterranean from the Alps. It is surrounded by four seas: on the west side above Corsica and Elba is the Ligurian; from Elba down to Sicily, the Tyrrhenian; between Sicily and the heel of Italy, the Ionian; and on the eastern side the Adriatic. Italy includes two of the largest islands in the Mediterranean, Sardinia a short distance south of Corsica and Sicily separated by the narrow Strait of Messina from the 'toe' of the mainland.

Italy is a land of contrasts ranging from the prosperous north to the much poorer south. Sardinia and Sicily are different worlds again. In the north, from the French border to La Spezia there is a string of marinas not dissimilar to the French coast. From La Spezia down to Rome a mixture of marinas and fishing harbours is found, and a few anchorages in the offlying islands; thereafter the marinas decrease drastically and small fishing harbours become the rule. In Sardinia there is a cluster of marinas around the fashionable Costa Smeralda in the north, but otherwise there are mostly fishing harbours and a few anchorages. In Sicily there are both fishing and commercial harbours with a few anchorages in the offlying islands. Around the tip and up the east coast of the mainland there are few harbours and anchorages until the prosperous north is reached where you will again find numerous marinas. Ashore facilities are good in the north and adequate in the south. In fishing harbours and remoter spots the locals will be friendlier, and while facilities may be fewer the will to help and find things is greater. You will rarely be unable to find good food ashore and in the smaller spots will come across delightful trattorias and ristorantes.

Malta The two islands, Malta and Gozo, have a total area of around 120 square miles. Like Gibraltar, it has traditionally been a base for yachts although there are a few harbours and bays to visit around the coast. At the principal harbour at Marsamxett there are good facilities for yachts and good and cheap cuisine ashore.

Yugoslavia The country is only some 370 miles long but the much indented coastline and numerous offshore islands add up to some ten times this figure. Apart from a 60 mile stretch of coast in the very south, a multitude of islands enclose sheltered and attractive cruising areas. These can be divided into four, beginning in the north. From Pula to Zadar the offlying islands enclose a large inland sea with a wealth of places to visit. From Zadar to Split the mainland coast is much indented and a chain of islands runs parallel to the coast. From Split to Dubrovnik is the most popular area with yet another archipelago. From Dubrovnik to the Albanian border there are no offshore islands, but the coast is much indented and a good cruising area all the same.

Yugoslavia has been making great efforts to attract yachts to its waters and there is now a chain of marinas along the coast, some purpose built, but others are harbours which have been provided with additional yacht facilities. The attraction of the country lies not in its marinas but in the multitude of tranquil anchorages around the islands and the mainland coast, where you can find a sheltered cove all to yourself. Ashore facilities are good in the marinas but not otherwise. Certainly you do not cruise in Yugoslavia to eat out or be entertained ashore; you come here to get away from all that.

Albania At the moment yachts cannot visit Albania and one should not attempt to do so, but there are signs that it may be getting ready to allow foreign yachts to cruise here in the future.

Greece The very irregular coastline and many islands make it impossible to calculate the length of the Greek coastline. Three seas hem it into the northeast corner of the Mediterranean. On the west, from Corfu in the north down to the bottom of the Peloponnessus, lies the Ionian sea. In the south the Cretan Sea encloses the crescent of Crete. North of Crete and locked in by mainland Greece and Asia Minor is the Aegean, peppered with islands. The regions within Greece are largely defined by the groups of islands rather than by the mainland coast. On the western side are the Ionian Islands from Corfu to Zante and the adjacent mainland coast. The Peloponnessus, separated from the mainland by the Gulf of Patras and the Gulf of Corinth, was completely severed by the construction of the Corinth Canal in 1893 to become a sort of large island. Crete and Karpathos and Kasos to its east close off the southern end of the Aegean. Within the Aegean Sea there are four distinct groups of islands: the Cyclades in the middle; the Dodecanese with Patmos at one end and Rhodes at the other lying in a chain along the coast of Asia Minor; the Eastern Sporades from Samos to Limnos lying north of the Dodecanese; and the Northern Sporades and Thasos and Samothraki in the northern Aegean. The broken coast and the islands scattered across the sea make up the best cruising area in the Mediterranean.

With only a few exceptions the whole of Greece offers superb cruising, although the eastern Aegean can be very windy in July and August when the *meltemi* blows. There are only a handful of marinas, most of them concentrated around Athens, so you will usually be in fishing harbours or anchorages. Parts of Greece can be crowded in the high season, but the greater part of it is not and out of high season there are considerably fewer yachts. Facilities ashore for yachts are few and far between, again mostly around Athens and

Corfu harbour with the high Pindus mountains of mainland Greece opposite

Piraeus. Eating out in Greece is more of an occasion than a fine gastronomic experience, though thoroughly enjoyable. In every village there is a simple taverna or a café that can whip up an omelette and salad, while in the more popular tourist spots the choice and standards are better, although not a culinary feast.

Turkey The largest country on the northern side of the Med, Turkey resembles a huge rectangular block wedged in among its neighbours. It is surrounded by four seas: the Black Sea on the north, the Sea of Marmara between the Bosphorus and the Dardanelles, the Aegean on the west, and the Mediterranean on the south. These effectively define the cruising areas; most activity is centred on the Aegean coast. The Black Sea and the Sea of Marmara are little cruised, and likewise the Mediterranean coast except between Fethiye and Antalya. Turkey has few offshore islands, but the many deep gulfs along the Aegean coast provide attractive cruising. There are a number of marinas around the coast, but mostly fishing harbours or anchorages. The majestic coast has steep mountainous slopes often thickly wooded in pine and the ruins of ancient cities are dotted everywhere. In the summer it can be crowded between Kusadasi and Antalya, but north and south of this the numbers of yachts decrease dramatically.

At the two oldest marinas, Kusadasi and Bodrum, facilities specifically for yachts can be found, but they are limited elsewhere. This is a country where the locals will have a go at making or repairing anything if given half a chance, and miracles are sometimes worked by the local blacksmith or the engineer in a tin shed on the outskirts of town. Eating out is a delight, with a tasty and varied cuisine presented with care and attention, and cheap.

Cyprus In 1974 Cyprus was partitioned into the Turkish Federated State of Cyprus in the north and the Republic of Cyprus in the south, the north containing the Turkish population and the south the Greek population. The Greek Cypriot government has introduced regulations prohibiting a yacht going from Turkish Cyprus to Greek Cyprus, although it may go from mainland Turkey to Greek Cyprus. Travel on land is also restricted; visitors must choose one side or the other.

Most yachts head for Larnaca marina, which is used as a base in the same way as Gibraltar and Malta. Although Cyprus is the third largest island in the Mediterranean, it has few safe natural anchorages and only a handful of man-made harbours. In the north Turkish military restrictions further limit where one can go. Consequently Cyprus is an island to visit and not one to cruise around.

Syria As one must get a visa in advance, and there are only a few man-made harbours along the straight sandy coast that can be visited, few yachts make the effort to cruise here.

Lebanon The bloody civil war effectively puts the coast off limits to yachts. Prior to the civil war a number of marinas operated and a few yachts visited the lovely Lebanese coast, but alas no more.

Israel The long, straight coast has no indentations or natural harbours. Yachts make for either Haifa or Tel Aviv.

Egypt Most yachts heading for Egypt are going through the Suez Canal and on to the Red Sea. A few yachts have gone up the Nile from Alexandria, but the practical and paperwork difficulties are considerable.

Libya You cannot enter without a visa and since these are not granted to yachtsmen you are effectively barred from going there.

Tunisia From Libya, the Tunisian coast turns sharply to the north until Cape Bon which lies only 90 miles across the Sicilian Channel from Sicily itself. Unlike the other North African countries, Tunisia has a much indented coast and a few offshore islands offering good cruising. The northern coast, from the Algerian border to Cape Bon, is relatively straight except for the Gulf of Tunis, and is surprisingly mountainous and fertile with many market gardens and citrus orchards. The eastern coast, from Cape Bon to the Libyan border, is mostly low-lying and as shallow water extends a considerable distance offshore it requires diligent navigation. The farther south you go along this coast, the more the vegetation recedes until the empty sands of the Sahara begin.

Several marinas have been built, but mostly yachts use fishing harbours or anchorages. Facilities are limited, and if you really want something it is better to nip across to Malta or Italy. Tunisian cuisine is basically Arabic; the ubiquitous cous-cous is its basis, with various sauces including the fiery hot *harissa*.

Algeria The coast stretches between Tunisia and Morocco for 760 miles; apart from a few large gulfs it is mostly straight and shelter must be found in man-made harbours. A few yachts do cruise here, but suspicious authorities and the paucity of harbours and anchorages deter most when the attractions of Spain are not far away.

Morocco A country that has been described as being surrounded by three seas: the Atlantic, the Mediterranean and the Sahara. It is some 250 miles from the Algerian border to the Strait of Gibraltar, but there are few harbours or anchorages. Most yachts just visit Tangier or Ceuta, the latter a Spanish enclave tucked just inside the Strait.

2
Weather Matters

To those raised in European waters there will in general be far more wind to be found in the Mediterranean, especially when the 'tradewinds' of the Aegean blow, or when the Adriatic bora rises sharply to full fury.

Alan Watts: *Wind Pilot*

Most people picture the Mediterranean as a deep blue sea ruffled by the occasional zephyr blowing out of an azure sky. The reality can come as something of a shock: it blows in the Mediterranean, and at times it can blow too much. In the Aegean the *meltemi* blows through July and August with some ferocity, often at Force 6 to 7 for days on end. Those ashore welcome the cooling wind and watch the yachts tossing at anchor, but the yachtsman curses the same wind shrieking through his rigging and prays for it to die down, especially if he is going north. At the other end of the Mediterranean the *levanter* hurtles through the Straits of Gibraltar, making it difficult even for ships going east to get through, and causing eddies over the Rock that complicate aircraft landings. The next day it is calm, and bewildered yachtsmen at either end of the Mediterranean get ready to motor out onto a mill-pond.

But if there are strong winds in the Mediterranean, and calms too, they are predictable for the most part. The beginning and end of the *meltemi* in the Aegean, its strength and direction, has been plotted since antiquity. Our *meltemi* (from the Turkish meaning bad-tempered) and the ancients' *etesians* (from the Greek *etios* meaning annual), were used by the plump merchant ships to sail south, where they waited until the autumn southerlies to come north again. Many of the big merchant fleets of the Middle Ages were prohibited to leave harbour at certain times of the year, until the bad winter weather had gone. In the western Mediterranean the sea breeze reigns supreme and small ships could safely tramp along the coast, 'buying one's butter at Villefranche, vinegar at Nice, oil and bacon at Toulon' (Braudel).

The idea that the Mediterranean summer is one of light zephyrs on a calm sea is a confusion concerning the predictable patterns of the season. A settled summer where thermal winds predominate does not mean a summer without strong winds. The blue sea can be quickly covered with whitecaps and steep seas whipped up by a wind blowing out of a clear azure sky.

The Sahara and the Atlantic

The climate of the Mediterranean, of settled sunny summers and violent wet winters, revolves around the forces generated by these two neighbours: the empty sandy wastes of the Sahara and the grey waters of the Atlantic. In the summer the Sahara acts as a giant weather incubator, bringing the clear azure sky and hot sun that bathes the sea and the land bordering it. The sands are a gigantic heat sink that give rise to powerful thermal winds. Out in the Atlantic the Azores high blocks depressions from descending into the Mediterranean and the cyclonic situation is virtually stable, on the large scale. In the winter the Atlantic dominates, sending depressions down into the Mediterranean through the Rhone Valley or straight through the Straits of Gibraltar, and with the depressions comes rain and violent, unpredictable weather.

The contrast between summer and winter is difficult for the northern mind to imagine, and as Ferdinand Braudel points out in his detailed study of the Mediterranean, 'the early Orientalist painters created an enduring false impression with their glowing palettes'. Today holiday companies create similar impressions with their glossy colour photographs. Braudel goes on to describe the fortunes of one Fromentin, a 19th century traveller escaping south to what he fondly believed was a mild, sunny winter in the Mediterranean. In October 1869, Fromentin, leaving Messina by boat, noted, 'grey skies, cold wind, a few drops of rain on the awning. It is sad, it could be the Baltic'. Earlier, in February 1848, he had fled towards the Sahara from the persistent grey mists of the Mediterranean winter: 'there was no interval that year … between the November rains and the heavy winter rains, which had lasted for three and a half months with hardly a day's respite'. All natives of Algiers must at one time or another have had occasion to see newcomers aghast at the torrential downpours over the city. (Braudel: *The Mediterranean and the Mediterranean World in the Age of Philip II*)

In spring and autumn the climate hovers between the Atlantic and Sahara influences. In the spring the Sahara effect works its way west and north bringing sun and warmth to the European shores. In the autumn the Atlantic influence is more violent as depressions swerve down through the Mediterranean, bringing gales and rain deep into the eastern region with little warning after the soporific summer.

I will concentrate here on the summer weather patterns because that is when you are likely to be sailing: most boats are laid up by October or November.

Winds

In the early days wind and weather were synonymous. The two words became almost interchangeable in English, a relationship which survives still in names such as 'weathervane' for a device which does no more in itself than indicate wind direction. When winds had a visible purpose and moved ships and mills or winnowed the grain, they were held in great esteem. People prayed or whistled for them or even, if it seemed expedient, bought one from an aged crone who sold the best ones cheap.

Lyall Watson: *Heaven's Breath*

Anticyclones and Pressure Differences
In Britain and northern France the changeable Atlantic climate predominates, bringing variable summer weather. In eastern Europe and Russia the extremes of the Continental climate dictate the weather. The Mediterranean climate is separated to a degree from the Atlantic and Continental systems by the mountains fringing its northern edge: those of the Iberian Peninsula, and of the French, Swiss and Austrian Alps, and the Balkans. In the summer the Mediterranean locks into its own cyclonic system that produces the predictable summers. From early June until late September a high pressure system sits over the central southern Mediterranean, affecting the weather from the Straits of Gibraltar to the Aegean. This stable weather pattern along with the Azores high halts the ingress of depressions into the Mediterranean, with the result that all weather is local weather.

those raised in European waters there will in general be far more wind to be found in the
Mediterranean"

Most of this local weather is thermally induced with sea breezes providing the important winds for the yachtsman. What must be realised is the scale of these sea breezes, generated by the hot southern sun. They are not always the light zephyrs familiarly associated with a sea breeze, but can be fresh to strong winds up to Force 6. By funnelling and deflection along a shore they can occasionally reach gale force.

When the land warms to a temperature above that of the water it creates a pressure difference that draws a breeze in from the sea. As the land warms up it will normally begin to blow about midday and will continue until dusk, reaching its peak around 3–5 pm local time. Occasionally a sea breeze will be opposed by another wind blowing directly or obliquely off the land so that its strength is decreased. Alternatively it can increase a wind already blowing onshore, rising to a late afternoon peak that may reach gale force.

The mechanics of the sea breeze hold good throughout the Mediterranean summer (with some important exceptions described later). Thus nights are usually calm a few hours after dusk. In the early morning there may be a light breeze blowing off the land at perhaps 10 knots but usually less. Around midday or early afternoon the sea breeze will fill in and blow until dusk or just after. It is real gentlemen's sailing with calm nights and a brisk afternoon breeze for a short passage along the coast. Should the prevailing wind be in the wrong direction then you can choose to get up early and motor to your next port of call, or thrash to windward in the afternoon – but gentlemen don't go to windward, do they?

It all sounds delightfully simple to rely on the sea breeze to explain winds in a Mediterranean summer, but in practice the picture is much more complicated. Local topography drastically affects what happens to winds, sometimes stopping them and sometimes accelerating them down valleys or around headlands. Lee eddies caused by a gulf or a large bay can reverse winds. The wind 20 miles off a coast can be radically different from that inshore. Special winds like the *mistral* or *bora* can violently over-ride the prevailing sea breeze. And in the Aegean a pressure difference between the monsoon low centred over Pakistan and the Azores high pulls the *meltemi* in a large arc from the Black Sea through the Aegean to Crete and Rhodes.

Let us look at some of the factors that complicate the picture.

Coastal Effects

Some sailors praise long tradewind passages where the wind blows constantly from the same direction at the same strength. Rolling from gunwale to gunwale for several thousand miles is not my cup of tea, but then tradewind sailors curse the variability of the wind around the Mediterranean. For me it is these very changes which gives it interest, and given a little knowledge of how the land affects the wind's direction and strength, you can pit your wits against a wind puzzle that is as complex as a chess game. Moving air takes the path of least resistance, so where there is high land near the coast it is deflected, funnelled and channelled according to the shape of the land.

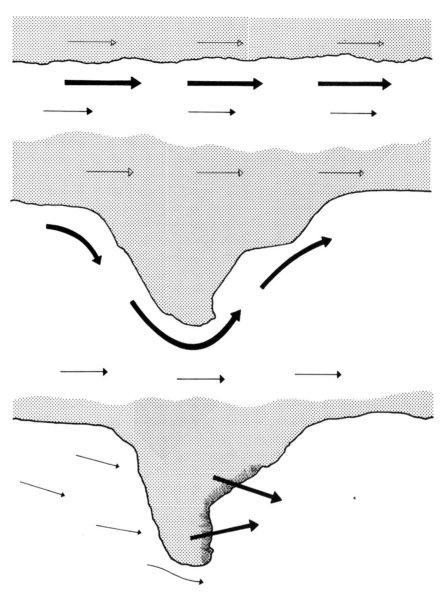

...tal effects that modify the wind ...tion and strength found on the open

Wind blowing onto or along a coast will freshen close to the shore. The land offers more resistance than the sea, and where there are high cliffs or mountains the wind is simply blocked from blowing over the land.

Around a headland wind will increase and change direction to take the easy path around the land. What can happen is that around, say, a small island, the wind will follow the shore and curve right round so that on the opposite side it is blowing from the opposite direction.

When the wind increases above a certain strength it may start to gust over the headland. On the windward side close to the headland there will be light winds while on the lee side there will be strong gusts, often 2 or 3 Forces more than the wind at sea.

25

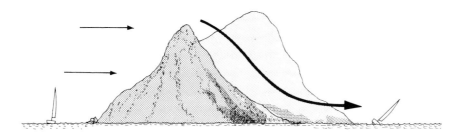

Wind gusting off the lee side of high land can be significantly stronger than the wind over the open sea.

Wind gusting into the lee of the land can also occur off a high shore or across islands: the wind literally falls off the steep lee side with considerable strength. It will usually take the path of least resistance down a valley or over the lower hills. The North European yachtsman unused to the phenomenon of strong gusts on the lee side of capes and islands should take every care in this situation – the gusts can shred sails.

Where the wind blows into a channel or gap, say between islands, it will tend to follow the channel rather than blow across the land, and so it is channelled and speeded up. It can also bend round and, for example, a useful beam wind outside can become a headwind in a restricted channel, or variable. You may then have to short-tack or motor to get through.

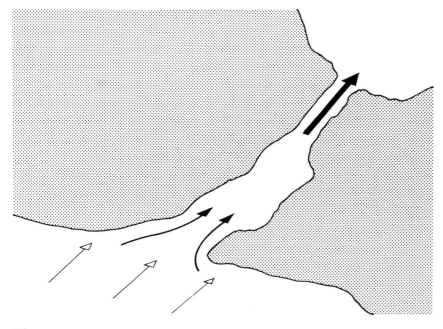

Wind effects from channelling.

Where a wind is establishing itself against an opposing wind there will be a buffer zone of variables in between, which can be several miles or as little as a hundred metres across. Across a narrow buffer zone the incongruous sight of a boat running one way approaching another boat running in the opposite direction can take a minute or two to comprehend.

Coriolis Effect In North Europe sea breezes are not usually strong enough to be affected by this, but in the Mediterranean they are. The Coriolis effect results from the earth spinning on its axis and deflecting objects from a straight path: it has to be taken into account when a shell is fired from a field gun, for example. In the northern hemisphere the deflection is towards the right so that winds are deflected slightly to the west. This westerly component can be detected in the prevailing winds of the Mediterranean where a 'pure' onshore sea breeze blowing onto say the Costa Blanca would blow directly onshore from the southeast but is in fact deflected to come from the south.

With this basic armoury of information we can look at the behaviour of a prevailing wind. On the map I show what happens to the prevailing wind around Levkas, one of the Ionian Islands in Greece. The wind out at sea on a typical summer's day is a northwesterly Force 4 to 5.

Other Winds *(See page 3)*

Sea breezes and the modifications produced by the local topography make up the bulk of the winds that yachts will encounter in the Mediterranean, but some others, mostly also thermally induced, need to be known and understood, particularly the violent ones.

Anabatic winds The wind flows uphill when the slopes of mountains are warmer than the valleys or plains: the effect occurs in the early morning when the upper slopes get the sun and the lower slopes and valleys are shaded. As it rarely exceeds 5 knots it does not pose the same threat as the katabatic wind.

Katabatic winds At night, when the tops of the mountains and hills cool before the land and sea at the bottom, the air flows down the slopes. On the way it gathers momentum as more air cools and adds to the wind. Where it is funnelled by a valley it can reach Force 6–7 at sea level. Katabatic winds arrive without warning, often blowing in from the opposite direction of the prevailing daytime wind. They are most likely in spring and autumn but where they are known to occur frequently it pays to take special care. In most cases they are over in a couple of hours, but off mountains such as the high Taurus in eastern Turkey they have been known to blow at Force 7–8 for most of the night.

Coastal slope winds are similar to katabatic winds but on a grander scale. They occur where a large land mass is cooled by continental air on one side and has a warm sea on the other. The classic example is the *bora* in the Adriatic where the wind blows from the cold Balkans onto the warm Adriatic; others are the *vardarac* that blows down into the Gulf of Thessaloniki, and the *bora* that blows into the Black Sea. These winds are to be avoided at all costs. They regularly reach gale force and wind speeds up to 60 knots have been recorded. The danger lies not just in their violence but also in the suddenness with which they arrive: 50 knots of wind can build up in under an hour, out of a clear sky. Fortunately they are not frequent in the summer, being predominantly a winter wind, but they do blow frequently in the autumn.

Mountain gap winds are big brother to funnelled winds. Cold air, often from a depression, is bottled up by a mountain range until it finds a gap to escape through. The classic example is the *mistral*, which lets the cold Atlantic air piling into France in the wake of a cold front out through the Rhone Valley. The *mistral* shoots out into the Gulf of Lions under a clear sky with little or no warning, often blowing up to Force 9–10 in the winter.

It spreads fan-wise from the Gulf of Lions across to the Balearics and to Sardinia and Sicily. Strabo, the Greek geographer, described it as 'an impetuous and terrible wind which displaces rocks, hurls men from their chariots, breaks their limbs and strips them of their clothes and weapons'. Other mountain gap winds are the *levanter* through the Straits of Gibraltar, and the *tramontana* which empties cold European air into the Gulf of Genoa.

Desert winds that blow off the Sahara bring hot air to Europe. The classic desert wind is the *sirocco*, which is pulled off the desert when a series of lows pass eastward across the Mediterranean. As it crosses the sea it picks up moisture, bringing a leaden sultriness to the European shore. It is said that if the *sirocco* blows for more than three days in Sicily all inexplicable crimes of passion are excused: certainly it produces an oppressive and un-pleasant atmosphere, as well as depositing the red sand of the Sahara over everything. The *sirocco* is most common in the spring but occurs at other times as well; it can blow a gale but normally is less than this. In different parts of the Mediterranean it is known by different names: *levante* in Spain, *leveche* in Morocco, *chergui* in Algeria, *chili* in Tunisia, *ghibli* in Libya, *khamsin* in Egypt, and *sharav* in Israel.

The meltemi – a special case Throughout July and August, and to a lesser extent in June and September, the *meltemi* (*meltem* in Turkey) blows from the Black Sea down through the Aegean to Crete and Rhodes and the adjacent Turkish coast as far as Finike. In July and August it is often Force 6–7 with stronger gusts off high land. The *meltemi* is a result of a pressure gradient between the Azores high and the monsoon low over Pakistan. The coastal effects previously described cause it to curve round to blow from the west into the gulfs along the Turkish coast, and be funnelled and channelled over and around the islands of the Aegean. It has a thermal component, in that it will often die down in the early morning and like the sea breeze is at its strongest in the late afternoon.

Waterspouts A waterspout is a whirlwind vortex which agitates the water surface, send-ing up spray, and with a funnel cloud connecting it to the cloud above in a dark column. Although a threatening sight, they seem to represent a minor hazard to yachts: I cannot track down one yachtsman who has been hit by one although sightings are common enough; in one case a small waterspout came as close as a hundred metres. The base of a waterspout is very narrow, from a few metres across to perhaps an average in the order of 20 metres, around which there is an area of agitated water. This is not salt water but fresh, condensation from inflowing air falling back into the sea from the waterspout. The darker the appearance, the more vigorous the winds around it. Although the winds driving a waterspout must be considerable (think of what the land equivalent, the tornado, can do), as I have mentioned the phenomenon seems to pose little danger to yachts. One of the few documented cases seems to indicate that the amount of water suddenly dumped on a boat may be a bigger hazard than the wind itself. The White Star liner *Pittsburgh* was hit by a huge waterspout in mid-Atlantic in 1923: so many tons of water were dumped on her so suddenly that her bridge was wrecked, the crow's nest and her officers' quarters flooded, and she had to heave-to in a calm sea while the damage was repaired.

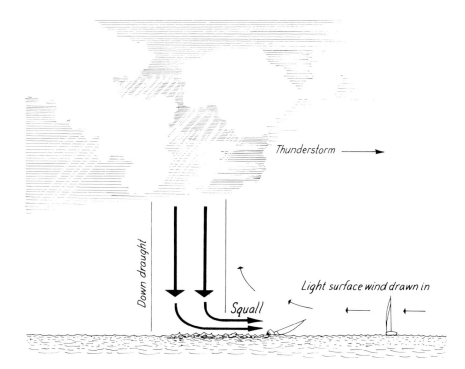

Thunderstorm ⟶

Down draught

Squall

Light surface wind drawn in

...cal wind pattern of a thunderstorm.

Thunderstorms In unstable air when cumulus and cumulo-nimbus clouds form thunderstorms, there can be a severe squall produced by the rush of rain falling down through the cloud. With a thunderstorm there will be little warning of such a wind apart from the visual cloud and falling rain, and thunder and lightning. You can roughly gauge your distance from a thunderstorm by dividing the number of seconds between the lightning and hearing the thunder by five, which gives the distance in miles. Typically the downdraft produced by the rain arrives in seconds with the peak gusts at the very beginning of the squall. As these gusts commonly reach Force 6–7 and may produce 50–60 knot winds, a thunderstorm is not something to be trifled with. If you appear to be on a collision course with a thunderstorm (this can be difficult to determine) it is prudent to take precautions and get the sails off, or at least reef drastically. The squall from a thunderstorm may last only minutes or it may go on for several hours during a big storm.

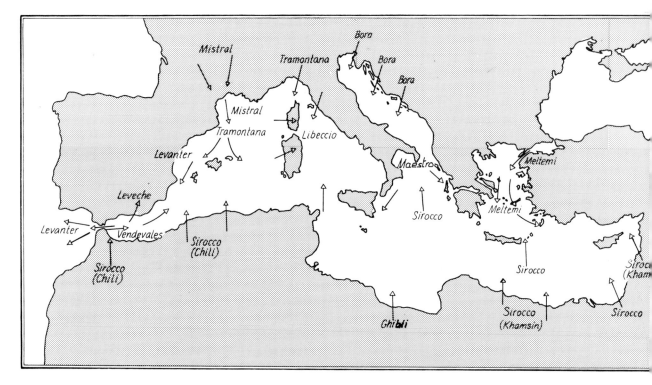

Local names for the winds in the Mediterranean. The arrows do not indicate the frequency, only direction.

Prevailing Summer Winds

Gibraltar The winds are predominantly from the east (*levanter*) or the west (*vendeval*), these two winds accounting for nearly 80% of the total.

Spain The onshore sea breeze is the predominant summer wind with a fair percentage of calms. The sea breeze has a westerly deflection so that in some places it blows parallel to the coast. There may be a light land breeze blowing off the land at night. The *levanter* also blows, from the northeast in the Gulf of Valencia and from the east in the Alboran Channel. In the Balearics the breezes are variable with no one direction prevailing.

France The onshore sea breeze is often deflected to blow along the coast and can be fresh in summer. A local *mistral* blows frequently enough in the summer for it to be watched carefully, especially where it is known to gust off the land. Along the Cote d'Azur the *mistral* is less in evidence and the onshore sea breeze predominates.

Corsica and Sardinia The sea breeze also predominates here, and is strengthened by channelling off Cape Corse, through the Strait of Bonifacio and around Cagliari. Off the high mountains of the islands there can be strong squalls, especially when the *libeccio* blows.

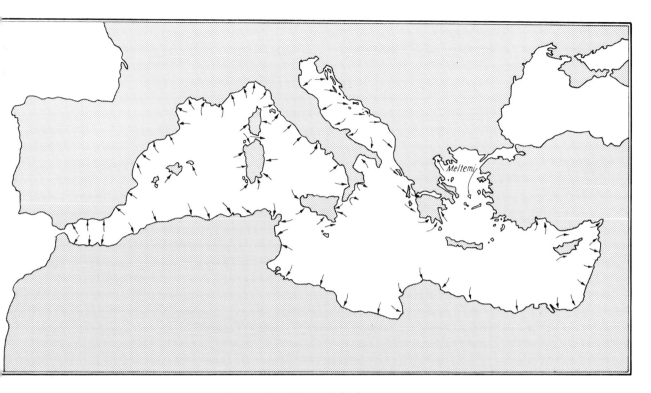

sea breeze wind direction close to the coast. These winds are much modified by the local topography by other special winds such as the levanter and the meltemi. Winds 20 miles off the coast will often different to the coastal winds.

Italy West coast The sea breeze blowing onshore is the predominant wind although there are often periods of calm. The *tramontana* from the northeast and north occasionally blows but not at its winter strength. The *sirocco* may also blow although it is most frequent in the spring.

East coast The prevailing winds are northerlies which follow the contours of the coast. There are frequent calms and in the spring and summer southerlies also blow. The *bora* does not blow as strongly onto the Italian coast as it does through the Yugoslavian islands.

Yugoslavia The predominant wind is the westerly sea breeze, but it is so channelled by the islands and mountains that it can blow from the southwest, south and northwest depending on the local topography. The *bora* can blow in the summer, and there are often katabatics off the mountains at night. The *sirocco* blows in the spring and autumn.

Greece In the Aegean the *meltemi* dominates, coming from the northeast in northern Greece and turning in an arc down through the Cyclades to blow from the west around Rhodes. In late July and August it can blow at considerable strength with stronger gusts on the lee side of capes and islands. In the Ionian the sea breeze blows in from the northwest, becoming west and southwest around the Pelopenessus. In mountainous areas a katabatic may blow at night.

31

Turkey The *meltem* blows down the coast and into the gulfs as far south as Finike. Further east and south the sea breeze predominates, with a consistent land breeze at night and sometimes through the morning. Around the Taurus there are violent katabatic winds at night.

Cyprus Sea and land breezes predominate, often blowing along the coast.

Syria, Lebanon and Israel The sea breeze predominates, blowing onto the coast; it is deflected along the coast in many places so that the prevailing wind tends to be southwesterly.

Egypt and Libya Again sea breezes dominate, with the coast deflecting them to blow from the northwest and west.

Tunisia The predominating sea breeze is much deflected to follow the contours of the coast. Along the north coast it blows from the west, but in the gulfs can blow from northwest through to northeast. In the Sicilian Channel the wind is mainly from the west but can also blow strongly from the east. On the east coast of Tunisia the sea breeze blows onshore from the east and northeast.

Algeria and Morocco The sea breeze predominates blowing onshore from anywhere between northwest and northeast. It can blow at some strength owing to the strong thermal effects generated here. A strong *sirocco (chili)* can blow off the land depositing sand everywhere. In the Straits of Gibraltar the winds are as for Gibraltar.

Local Names for Mediterranean Winds

These names do not indicate frequency, but often they are specially named because they disturb the normal wind patterns or are exceptionally violent.

Arifi Strong *sirocco* in Morocco.

Bise Cold, dry northeasterly in the Languedoc–Rousillon region.

Bora Violent katabatic type of wind blowing off the Balkans (and the Karst and Dinaric Alps) into the Adriatic.

Borasco Gale with squalls and thunderstorms in Italy; predominantly westerly and southwesterly.

Borini Small *bora* on the Italian Adriatic coast.

Bura Bora

Chergui Warm dry *sirocco* in Morocco.

Chili Hot, dry *sirocco* in Tunisia and Algeria.

Chom Hot, dry southerly in Algeria.

Dzhani Warm, dry southerly in North Africa.

Etesians Ancient name for the *meltemi*, no longer commonly used.

Gharbi Strong, moist, dust-laden southwesterly in Morocco; brings the 'red rain' to France, Italy and Greece. Known as the *Gharbis* in Italy and Greece.

Ghibli Strong *sirocco* in Tunisia.

Gregale Strong northeasterly blowing over the Tyrrhenian and Ionian Seas to Malta; associated with a *bora*. Also called *grecale* – the 'Greek wind'.

Imbat Sea breeze in North Africa, also the local name for the *meltem* in the Gulf of Iszmir.

Khamsin Hot, dry *sirocco* in Egypt.

Levante Strong east to northeasterly winds blowing onto the Spanish coast. Build up a big swell across the comparatively long fetch.

Levanter Easterly winds blowing through the Straits of Gibraltar.

Leveche Hot, dry dust-laden southeasterly blowing onto southern Spain.

Llevantades Gales from the northeast in eastern Spain.

Libeccio West or southwesterlies in Italy. Can be strong and accompanied by squalls and
    thunderstorms.
Maestral Northerlies in France.
Maestrale Cold, dry *mistral* type wind in the Gulf of Genoa.
Maestro Sea breeze in the Adriatic and the Greek Ionian. Also *maistro*.
Marin Warm, humid, dust-laden southerlies in the Gulf of Lions. Similar to the *leveche*.
Meltemi Strong northerlies becoming westerly in the Aegean. Known as the *meltem* in
    Turkey and the *etesians* to the ancient Greeks.
Mestral Northerlies in Spain similar to the *maestral*.
Mistral Cold, dry, strong winds blowing out of the Rhone Valley into the Gulf of Lions,
    often as far as the Balearics and Sardinia.
Ponente Westerlies in Italy and Greece.
Sharav Hot, dry *sirocco* in Israel.
Simoom Hot, dry, desert wind in North Africa. Literally means 'the poisoner'. Also
    simoon.
Sirocco Hot, dry, southerlies from North Africa. They pick up moisture over the sea to
    become humid and oppressive winds by the time they reach European shores.
Tramontana A *bora* which extends to Corsica and Sardinia.
Vardarac A *bora* type wind in the Aegean, especially the Gulf of Thessaloniki.
Vendeval Westerly winds in the Straits of Gibraltar. Also *vendevales*.

The sea

'Praise the sea, and stay on the land' says a Provencal proverb, and when beating to
windward in a Force 6 in the short steep swell of the Mediterranean, many of us might
echo similar sentiments.

Waves

It is always difficult to compare overall conditions and wave types for different areas.
Statistics on wave height, speed and period do not convey what a confused sea with a
cross-swell is like, and we must resort to description to get some idea. Most yachtsmen
agree that the Mediterranean generally produces steep waves with a very short period:
compared to longer waves, they make sailing to windward more uncomfortable and
difficult, let alone motoring into them, unless you have a big engine and a robust hull. An
Australian friend of mine put it differently: 'The trouble with the Mediterranean is the
waves. In the Pacific you've got a big long ocean swell; ten minutes on the way up to
make a cup of tea, ten minutes on the top to drink it, and ten minutes on the way down to
decide if you want another cup. Now your average Mediterranean wave is square, and
how's a bloke going to make a cup of tea let alone drink it on one of those?'

Close to the shore there will often be a confused swell, especially off a headland. Much
of the land drops sheer into the sea and keeps going straight down, with the result that a
swell setting onto it is simply reflected back. The resulting irregular waves can make it
worth keeping a mile or so offshore.

The other feature of the Mediterranean sea that can be surprising is the way the sea can
go from a millpond to a wave-tossed maelstrom in a very short time. You can set out
under engine in a flat calm and be blown into your next port reefed right down. Not only
can wind build up quickly, but the waves also.

One last word on waves. The Mediterranean is a small area of water in comparison to
the oceans, but it does not mean there are not large waves. The maximum wave height

from trough to crest is in the order of 14 metres, except in the centre of a hurricane where the massive winds can create waves over 24 metres high. In the Mediterranean, where there is sufficient fetch waves can reach substantial heights; 12 metres being the maximum recorded, in the channel between Sicily and Tunisia.

Tides and Currents

It is common knowledge that the nearly land-locked Mediterranean is virtually tideless. At Gibraltar the tidal range at springs is around a metre whereas at the eastern end of the Mediterranean it is measured in tens of centimetres. In several other areas where the continental shelf (depth under 200 metres) extends out some distance, principally at the northern end of the Adriatic and the eastern coast of Tunisia, the otherwise barely noticeable tides are amplified to as much as a 2 metre range.

Although tides can for the most part be discounted, the currents in the Mediterranean should not be. A great deal of water is lost by evaporation and not replaced by rainfall or the water from rivers. The massive shortfall flows in from the Atlantic through the Straits of Gibraltar and then circulates in a roughly anti-clockwise direction around the Mediterranean. However its complex shape with so many major peninsulas and islands means that the overall pattern of the current is radically altered by the land. Furthermore, a current can be halted or even reversed if the wind blows strongly and consistently from the opposing direction.

All that the yachtsman can do is consult the relevant pilot book and guesstimate the rate and direction of the current. Do not assume that currents can be disregarded, even on passages of 30 miles or so. Depending on where you are, and even from day to day, they can make a significant difference to your dead reckoning calculations. I recently sailed down the outside of Evia in Greece and on one 30 mile passage was set 5 miles to the west of my course: so it pays to keep an eye on things where you know there are strong currents.

In places such as the Straits of Messina between Sicily and the toe of Italy, and the narrow channel between Evia and mainland Greece, the currents are channelled to flow at considerable rates and can give rise to overfalls and whirlpools. The infamous Charybdis in the Straits of Messina, that threatened to suck Odysseus and his fellow voyagers to the bottom, is still there, although much reduced in size and force after an earthquake altered the submarine topography. Less well known are the complex currents in the Evia Channel that so bewildered Aristotle he is reputed to have thrown himself into the waters in despair. Around headlands and in narrow channels in other parts of the Mediterranean you may not come across renowned whirlpools, but you can encounter overfalls and broken water when the wind is against the current in a similar way to the disturbed water of wind against tide. Unfortunately there is no tide to turn so you must simply plug on.

Sea Levels The small tidal range means that for all intents and purposes you can take the depth of water under your keel to be the depth of water there six hours later. However there are certain conditions that can alter the sea level by up to a metre. If the wind blows consistently from the south or north for weeks on end, into or out of an enclosed gulf or bay, it can create an uphill slope decreasing the sea level in one place and increasing it in another. The classic example of this is Venice, where strong and consistent southerlies can push the waters of the lagoons up into the ground floors of the venerable old buildings of the city. A similar phenomenon can occur in northern Greece. Along the south coast of Sicily a phenomenon known as the *marrobio* can drastically alter the sea level. It is a form of seiche and has been recorded in Tunisia, the Balearics and the Gulf of Corinth as well as

Sicily. It is a 'tidal' wave which quickly and smoothly raises the level of the water by up to a metre and then recedes again in a few minutes. The cycle may continue for a few minutes or a few hours. It is said to be connected with general meteorological conditions in the Mediterranean as a whole, principally humid conditions, a falling barometer and the onset of southerlies, but no-one is really sure of exactly when or why a *marrobio* occurs. Its main effect is likely to be on your mooring lines and gangplank.

Bad Weather

Winter in the Mediterranean comes as a malevolent mocking of the settled sunny summer. It rains. It hails. It snows. Bone-chilling winds cause the temperatures to plummet and set grandmothers to knitting woollen sweaters for grandchildren. Depressions roar in from the Atlantic bringing storms that break down harbour walls and rip the tiles off roofs. The violence of a Mediterranean winter is wholly unexpected by those who have not experienced one before. In spring the winter rapidly recedes, earlier in the east than farther west and north. In the autumn winter arrives quickly and violently with torrential rain and thunderstorms, although there is usually a brief respite in November, a sort of Mediterranean 'Indian summer' (to jumble up two disparate parts of the world).

Although it is possible to sail in the winter, most yachts are laid up by November. The southeastern part of the Mediterranean is the most popular for those determined to potter in the winter, but even here passages need to be planned with a port of refuge in easy reach. In the western Mediterranean few yachts venture out in the winter except for day-sailing; on longer passages they would expect to get a battering.

In the spring and autumn the sailing can be superb although an eye must still be kept on the weather, especially in March and October. At the beginning and end of the summer the air temperatures are not up to the stifling highs of July and August, and in spring the land is covered in a profusion of wildflowers and a green unimaginable three months later.

Depressions

In the winter and to a lesser extent in spring and autumn, the winds are produced not by thermal effects but by cyclonic systems. The Atlantic is the important influence on winds then. Most depressions coming in from the Atlantic tend to follow predictable routes, although in the eastern Mediterranean their direction and speed become less predictable: they may remain stationary and then speed off again for no apparent reason.

On the north side of the Mediterranean lows enter through the Rhone Valley or through the Alps into the Gulf of Genoa. In the Gulf of Genoa a depression will frequently deepen and then move eastwards, bringing gale force winds and torrential rain to the eastern Mediterranean. The Genoa lee cyclone gives rise to some of the strongest winds and frequently halts shipping in its vicinity. Depressions also come through the Straits of Gibraltar and move eastwards, or from the south across Algeria or Tunisia.

The highest winter gale frequency occurs in the Gulf of Lions with an average of 12 gales in the winter. In the Balearics the average is four, as in the sea area between Sardinia and Sicily. In the Ionian the average is also four; in the Aegean it increases to eight. While these figures give us an idea of gale frequencies, they do not necessarily represent the frequency of gale force *winds*. Small disturbances that hardly nudge the barometer can cause violent winds with little or no warning. Large thunderstorms can generate 50–60 knot gusts. And a strong breeze can be funnelled through a gap causing gale force winds. As in the summer, the local topography plays havoc with wind direction and velocity.

Weather Forecasts

On the whole, prediction becomes less reliable the farther east you go. Gibraltar, Spain, France and Italy broadcast forecasts on the medium waveband that provide a reliable guide to the weather. The Greek forecast will give an indication of gales but its local predictions can be way out. Most marinas post a weather forecast, and after the television news at night there is frequently a synoptic chart shown as part of the weather news. Other sources of weather information are the port police or harbourmasters, although the results can be amusing: in Crete I asked the port police for a weather forecast whereupon one of them strolled across to the window, looked outside and with a wave of his arm told me it would be 'o.k.'.

The difficulties of weather prediction in the Mediterranean were vividly illustrated for me recently. A 70 foot yacht was sitting in the Ionian with its weather facsimile receiver on, monitoring the conditions for the right moment to cross to Sicily. Eventually the big day arrived and the yacht left with light northeasterlies predicted. A few hours later it returned having been battered by strong westerlies. For a while it looked as if the crew might put a weatherfax mooring block down in the Ionian.

The Big Bad Four

There are many strong winds which blow frequently in different parts of the Mediterranean and which are to be feared, but there are four which merit special consideration: the *levanter*, the *mistral*, the *bora* and the *meltemi*.

Levanter The easterly which blows through the Strait of Gibraltar where it is funnelled into the Atlantic. It is often at gale strength and may blow for a week or more; most frequent in the winter, it occurs in all seasons and is accompanied by heavy rain, violent squalls (especially in the Straits) and sometimes thunderstorms. The *levanter* can cause violent eddies where it meets the land.

Mistral The violent wind that blows into the Gulf of Lions as far as the Balearics in the west and Sardinia and Sicily in the southeast. When it blows down the Spanish coast it is known as the *maestral* or *mestral* and in the Balearics as the *tramontana*. Gusts can be as high as 70 knots during a violent *mistral* and often are 40 knots. In the midsummer it blows at near-gale strength on average of four days a month, and sometime during the summer will reach strong gale or storm force. In March, the worst month, it blows at gale force for an average of nine days in the month, with gusts far in excess of gale force. The *mistral* blows with little warning out of a clear sky and this makes it especially dangerous – not for nothing is its name derived from the Latin *magistralis*, meaning 'masterly'.

Bora The predominantly winter wind that blows down into the Adriatic off the Balkans. It frequently blows at gale force with gusts exceeding 60 knots. On average it blows 40 days of the year with November and March being the worst months. From May through August the incidence is one day a month or less, rising gradually to five days in November. The *bora* gives little warning and has been recorded as going from a calm to 50 knots in 15 minutes – enough said.

Meltemi The wind that blows throughout the Aegean in July and August. Although it is rarely above gale force over the open sea, gusts off the land can be stronger. Its danger is not so much from its violence as the fact that it is likely to be encountered by a large number of yachts in the summer: if you are in the region it is difficult to escape it. The *meltemi* is a result of a stable pressure gradient, but it is also diurnal wind being strongest in the late afternoon and weakest in the morning. However, it may also blow unabated day and night for several days, at its worst.

of the things the yachtsman has to
used to is wind arriving suddenly and
great force with little or no warning.
n be perfect sailing weather one
ite and a gale of wind the next.

3
Harbours

Tassos would tell me that the best afternoon's entertainment was watching a flotilla come into harbour for the first time. The other locals would be alerted, Tassos would take his favourite seat in the taverna and order a bottle of ouzo, ready to watch a hilarious and completely free circus performed by tyro skippers on flotilla yachts and the anxious ringmaster (me) sprinting around the quay attempting to minimise collisions and disentangle lines. I had to be something of a cross between mime artiste and a traffic officer, signalling when to drop the anchor (imaginary object thrown into the water), when to put the engine into neutral (hand drawn across throat), when to go astern (hands frantically back-pedalling), and when to give a little forward power (inch shown between thumb and forefinger). Shouting at the incoming boat was useless as all on board were invariably shouting at one another and running around the decks, tripping over ropes and dropping fenders into the water.

When a boat charged at the quay as if to savage the spectators, Tassos and the locals would give a cheer to urge me on as I decided whether or not to be a human fender and cushion the impact. I've seen customers get up from quayside tables and retreat as a boat rushes at them apparently intent on climbing the quay and attacking – the white-knuckled skipper frozen in panic and unable to do anything but grasp the tiller and watch wide-eyed his impending doom. Tassos reckoned it was as close to gladiatorial combat as he was likely to see – those tyro skippers battling with their craft to get them berthed Mediterranean style.

To avoid becoming part of such a spectacle, the newcomer to the Mediterranean will have to work hard at perfecting this method of berthing. Going stern-to or bows-to with the anchor holding the boat off the quay is normal in the majority of harbours, so you are going to have to get used to it. Once you are in, you can sit back and watch the others.

iterranean blood-sport. Once you are safely berthed you can sit back and watch the others.

Everything in place and the crew ready with the berthing lines.

Boats get locked in, small boats get squashed by larger boats, people have to clamber over decks to get ashore. In this harbour, Cala Sta Maria in Italy, you can almost walk across the small harbour from boat to boat.

Mooring Alongside, and Stern or Bows-to a Quay

Alongside

In tidal waters it is often necessary to tie up parallel to a quay because of strong currents or because the harbour dries out. In the Mediterranean there is no such need, and there are in fact several disadvantages.

Mooring alongside is a complicated business when there are many boats to fit onto a quay. Some get locked in by others going alongside them, and small boats on the inside can get squashed by bigger ones on the outside. People have to clamber over your decks to get ashore, and back again after late night merriment. More boats can fit in with more privacy by berthing stern or bows-to the quay, and for this reason it is the common method used. In a few harbours you must go alongside so your anchor line (rode) doesn't obstruct the channel or a very small basin, or because there is a current. However, even where there is space to go alongside, for the reasons outlined below it is far far better not to.

Stern-to

The traditional method of berthing and perforce the only way for a large yacht. The size and weight of her chain and anchor, and the anchor handling gear needed, is all located up front and the gangplank is most easily rigged from the stern.

The advantages of going stern-to a quay are numerous. In many harbours there can be a surge, sometimes considerable, when the waves are running in a particular direction. When stern-to the boat is not bashing and scraping on the quayside as she will when alongside it. If things start to get bad you can ease off on the lines to the quay and pull yourself out on the anchor to ride to the surge the way a boat likes to. If you must get out, it is considerably easier to do so when stern-to than when alongside or bows-to.

It also keeps unwanted visitors from getting easy access to the boat, and I don't mean only the two-legged variety. Cockroaches and rats can be a big problem if they get aboard, and lying stern-to makes it difficult for them to do so. If you are alongside they can simply step aboard, not to mention stray dogs and cats or the occasional stray human being. If you raise the gangplank at night unwanted visitors of any variety find it difficult to get aboard. It gives you privacy and more security as well. Harbour urchins and others cannot press their grubby noses to the windows or peer down hatches as easily as they can when you are alongside.

Stern-to with a passerelle to get on and off.

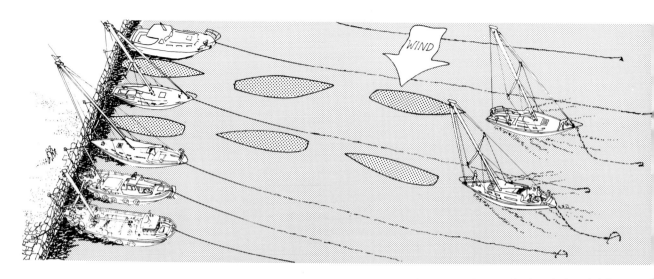

Berthing Mediterranean style. With a cross-wind you need to keep the boat slightly up-wind laying the anchor and then drop down into the berth as shown.

Bows-to

My first boat in the Mediterranean had no reverse gear so it was well nigh impossible to moor stern-to. The answer was to do what all the local fishing boats do and go bows-to. Now most small boats prefer to go bows-to the quay; some not so small craft do so as well and I've seen 13 and 14 metre yachts berthed this way. The principal reason for going bows-to is that it is much easier to drive a boat into a space by going forwards, the way it was designed to go, rather than astern. Boat designers don't design their craft to go backwards and consequently few boats do it well.

Going bows-to also keeps the cockpit private from quayside spectators, and since you are going to be living in the cockpit a lot of the time this is worthwhile. Another advantage is that you can get right up to the quay where the bottom slopes up to it or there is rubble or a ledge under the water next to the wall. If a boat is pushed onto the quay by an onshore wind less damage is likely from her bow hitting it than the stern or her rudder or self-steering gear.

This all makes good sense, but there are a couple of disadvantages as well. If the wind gets up while blowing onto the quay, a boat berthed bows-to will take it on the stern, where there is greatest hull windage and a large area for any chop to push her onto the quay. As well, the ground tackle used from the stern is lighter than the main anchor and chain. The really heavy mooring bitts and/or cleats are usually built into the bows; the fittings at the stern are likely to be smaller and unsuited to take heavy strains. By lying stern-to the boat is pointing into the wind and presenting the least hull windage, and the bows offer a smaller, more streamlined area for the sea to push on. A short chop plopping on the stern also makes a lot of noise, especially in an after-cabin. The other disadvantage is in leaving the berth: if you are stern-to you simply let off the stern lines and take in the anchor, giving a few bursts of forward power to help if necessary. When you are bows-to you must pull the boat out backwards, which can be a back-breaking task with the wind blowing onto the quay, and then turn her round. But more on this later. In practice the advantages of going bows-to outweigh the disadvantages, and most small boats opt for this method of berthing.

For handling the anchor line as you come in it is a wise policy to use a pair of gloves. Rope running out at speed can do a lot of damage to hands, even those used to it. When leaving, the gloves are just as important for hauling the anchor in, especially in dirty harbours where there may be a risk of infection if you cut or scrape your hand.

If you are on charter then you get whatever gear is on the boat. On flotilla follow the practice outlined by the flotilla leader: he or she won't thank you for rearranging their own carefully worked out technique. On a chartered bareboat, if the set-up looks clumsy or complicated then rearrange it into something familiar and straightforward.

Doing it

To describe the complete process of going stern-to or bows-to a quay involves many words for something that is easier to understand when you actually see it done – though it may also be harder to do than it appears. However, there are a number of tips that can be passed on, so here they are.

Preparation
The first few times you try to berth, you will not get it exactly right unless lady luck is squarely on your side. It is essential to judge just where you are going to put down the anchor and the ability to do this doesn't come automatically. The anchor should be laid three to four boat lengths straight out from the space you have selected. Take some time in the harbour selecting your space and getting the anchor, its chain or line, and the dock lines ready. Don't forget to put all the fenders out. If you size up a boat of similar length to your own that is already on the quay and estimate three to four boat lengths out from her you'll get some idea of where to drop the anchor, but on the first few occasions you will probably estimate short of the proper distance, due to a foreshortening of perspective when you are viewing a boat from this angle. It is better to place the anchor too far out than too close in.

When you are choosing your space assess the angles of the anchor lines from boats already berthed and especially those on either side of your chosen space. This is difficult to do and it is more than likely that on some occasions you are going to lay your anchor over another. Indeed, it is sometimes virtually impossible not to do so in a crowded harbour, or where an adjacent boat has laid out its anchor at an extreme angle. In that case place your own anchor as far out as possible: if you leave before the other boat then with

Everything must be ready in advance especially before entering a small and crowded harbour like this.

luck you can simply pick up your chain or rope from over the top of the other without snagging anything. If the other boat leaves first, she will most likely pick up your anchor, anchors being in that category of objects that have a magnetic attraction for one another, but hopefully it will be far enough out once disentangled to enable it to dig in again.

It is essential that you have everything set up on the right part of the boat and ready to use before even approaching your spot and lowering the anchor. Give your crew time by staying out in an uncrowded part of the harbour, or even outside it, until everything is set up, especially if they lack experience. If the anchor doesn't have much chain on it, tail a rope onto the end. If you will be going bows-to, tie an additional length of line to the one already on the anchor, in case you run short and end up in the embarrassing position of losing the bitter end in the water. Attempting to tie two lengths of line together when you are in the middle of berthing is a sure recipe for disaster. The bitter end should be made fast on the mooring strongpoints on the deck, just in case: you can adjust the final length later.

Have all your lines 'made up' (ends on their cleats): from bow or stern, you need one line on each side, with their inner ends led under the lifelines and put onto cleats. Keep a spare long line coiled and handy in case anything goes wrong and you need to get a line ashore. Fenders should be tied on, after a look at the boats next to your slot to get the right height to be effective. Have one large fender as a spare ready to be positioned in a hurry wherever it might be needed. Too often, as the boat races towards the quay fenders and lines are being hurriedly extracted from the cockpit locker, fingers are crushed as the locker lid slams shut, the cockpit resembles a rugby scrum, the skipper is worried, and as the boat gets closer a crowd of expectant onlookers can be seen to be growing on the quayside.

44

Stern-to

The principal difficulty with going stern-first is to hold a straight line into your chosen space. Twin-screw boats can get in anywhere – at least they should be able to. But single screw boats have to take into account the paddle-wheel effect of the propeller. A right-handed propeller will pull the stern around to port and a left-handed propeller to star-board. ('Handing' is the direction that a prop and its shaft turns, as one looks forward from the stern.) If you have an offset propeller pray for divine assistance. The rudder has little effect on this tendency unless you have got the boat going astern with a bit of speed on; even then she will often slew off, especially if there is a cross-wind.

While some say you need to get the boat going at a good clip some distance out from where you are going to drop the anchor, in practice this can turn out disastrously. Get the boat going with some way on and have someone reliable letting the anchor go and ensuring that its chain or rope runs out totally freely. In theory the anchor chain should hold the boat on a straight course, but in practice it doesn't, and if the anchor chain is tight and holding it will swing the stern violently one way or the other. The chain should not be snubbed until you are half a boat's length off the quay. A couple of bursts of forward power will effectively slow you down and the anchor can then be tightened in.

If the boat does not run back on a straight line, straighten her up by giving a short burst of power in forward gear with the helm well over to bring the bows round, then adjust the rudder position for backing, after the burst, and go astern again. On boats with wheel steering it helps to stand on the forward side of the wheel facing aft so you can drive in using the wheel like a car's steering wheel. Resist the temptation to put the helm (wheel or tiller) hard over to its extreme position: it will then only drag and lose effectiveness. Looking over the stern also gives you a clear view of what is going on rather than getting a crick in your neck from craning your head over your shoulders.

ddle-wheel effect of the propeller when going astern. (i) A left-handed proller pushes the bows to
board and (ii) a right-hand propeller pushes the bows to port.

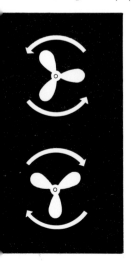

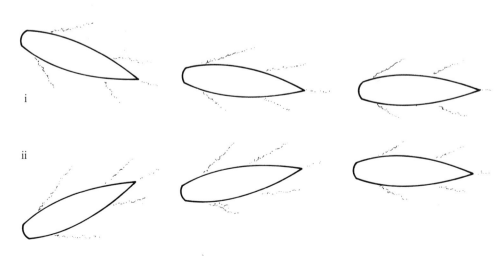

If you are off your approach line it is not necessary to take up the anchor and do a re-run of the whole thing, unless the anchor is in the wrong place or you are drastically out of line. If the anchor is on all chain you can confidently motor forward to the spot where the anchor was dropped and then start going astern again. If you are on chain and rope then a little more care is needed to guard against the rope getting around the keel, skeg, or worst of all the propeller.

Once you are nearly into a berth get a line ashore, the windward line first, and haul the boat in rather than using the engine. Make sure the quay end of the line is tied off so that you can adjust the lines from the boat. Tighten up on the anchor and you're there.

With a crosswind get the anchor down and then aim for the windward boat next to your slot as you approach slightly crabwise. At the last minute flick the wheel or tiller over and you will drop neatly down into the berth. If you attempt to head straight backwards into the berth the wind will simply blow you off sideways. As you get closer to the quay and the other boats the full force of a crosswind will be partially blocked making your task much easier.

Bows-to

Going in bows-first is essentially the same as going stern-to except you have fewer problems making the boat go where you want her to. The stern anchor should be ready to let go, with the line flaked out ready to run freely. Fasten the very end: it is surprising how many times an anchor line disappears over the stern if the end is not made fast, to the consternation of all on board. If you are short-handed it is a good idea to lead the line around a winch and feed it out from the cockpit. That way one person can control the anchor line and the helm and engine controls. Prehensile toes are useful for the latter.

Going bows-to is easier and more convenient for a small boat than going stern-to.

A stern anchor should not be oversize or have too much chain on it; if the gear is too heavy it cannot be used easily. In most harbours you will be in comparatively shallow water, probably 4−8 metres and often less, so a little chain and a long line are adequate for the purpose.

If you know the harbour is deep or that the bottom is not good holding, you can rig your main anchor and chain to do the job of a stern anchor. Tie a good, long, non-floating line to the end of the anchor chain and lead the end of the line from the bow roller back around the outside of the boat to the stern. The boat can now be taken in bows-first and in the appropriate spot for the anchor, the whole lot let go and hauled in from the stern. In theory this technique sounds full of pitfalls – the chain or line snagging the keel, skeg or propeller, the chain lying in a heap on the bottom, the chain fouling the anchor – but in practice this rarely occurs. When leaving after using this technique the boat can be hauled out stern-first and then when you are a safe distance out the line led forward to the bow roller and the whole lot hauled in from the bows. This way you are moving only a line about the boat rather than all the chain and an anchor, with the inevitable damage to the decks and fittings the latter would do. If it all sounds fraught with peril, then let me assure you I have used the main anchor in this way on numerous occasions and it has yet to foul up.

As with going stern-to it is best to get a little forward way on and then shift into neutral. A boat carries her way forward a considerable distance and applying reverse power has little effect on this forward momentum: the quay has a lot more stopping power. It is better to be going too slowly and to control the speed by putting the engine into gear and out again. For most of the manoeuvre you want to keep only a light tension on the line so as not to jerk the anchor out or put the boat off course. As you get near the quay slow the boat by less power and increased tension on the anchor line, letting a turn slip around the winch if need be.

On first attempts the most common fault is to have the boat moving too fast. Not only are you likely to hit the quay, but you will have no time to angle the boat in without damaging neighbouring boats. Once you have got a line to the quay pull the boat into position while tightening up on the stern anchor – it does your lungs and muscles good to haul in lines rather than leaning on the gear lever.

you get near to the quay, slow the ... t by increasing tension on the anchor ... e and get a line ashore as soon as ... ssible.

Setting up for bows-to mooring

The simplest system is to tie a plastic bucket on the after deck in the corner of the pushpit (stern rail) and keep the chain and line coiled in it. The anchor can hang on the pushpit, secured by elastic bungee cord; it can then be let go over the pushpit and the chain and line run out from the bucket. Make sure the deck and transom edge is protected by a stainless plate or wooden sacrificial strip, or if the chain/rope runs out over the top of the pushpit put a piece of plastic hose over the bar to protect it.

Some boats have more elaborate and elegant anchor handling arrangements for going bows-to: a short 'bowsprit' or boomkin over the stern with an anchor roller at the end keeps the chain and line clear of the transom. Several boats I have seen have even mounted a small anchor winch on the stern to handle the chain and line with minimum fuss. Others have the equivalent of a garden-hose reel with a brake on it to handle the line. Mounted on the pushpit, it facilitates letting go and reeling in the anchor line although it must always be getting in the way of other activities on the after deck.

Anchor stowage arrangements depend on the type of anchor. A Danforth can be stowed in a simple wooden box bolted onto a retroussé transom. A Bruce or CQR can be hung on stainless hooks welded onto the pushpit and the anchors secured with bungee or line. Some boats have room on the afterdeck for a small locker where anchor, chain and line can all be stowed out of sight.

Whatever system is adopted or worked out, it should above all be simple and easy to use. It is no use having a neat and 'yachty' looking arrangement if it is impractical. Dragging anchors, chain and ropes around a cockpit not only damages the boat but will most likely damage your fingers and toes as well – so keep it all simple and keep your anatomy out of the way.

Stern-to stowage. It may not look particularly 'yachty' but it works.

*...en quite large yachts will often elect to go bows-to rather than stern-to, though for the very large,
...rn-to is the only way.*

Getting out

Though this presents fewer problems than getting into a mooring slot, some of these can
be difficult. Leaving a stern-to berth is simply a matter of taking in the anchor cable and
occasionally motoring forward to keep position. But from a bows-to berth you should
use the engine as little as possible or not at all until the line and then the anchor are on
board, or you run the risk of getting the line around the propeller. Then you will be in the
unenviable position of having no engine and no anchor to let go – and an almighty panic
on your hands. In that event, as soon as you can, get the main (bow) anchor down, unless
as is likely you have drifted into another boat, the quay or aground – in which case you
might as well sit there until you have got things sorted out. Usually the only thing for it is
a swim to clear the propeller. Often you will have to cut the line off and for this a
breadknife is a good weapon. Profuse apologies to any boats you have drifted down on
will also be in order.

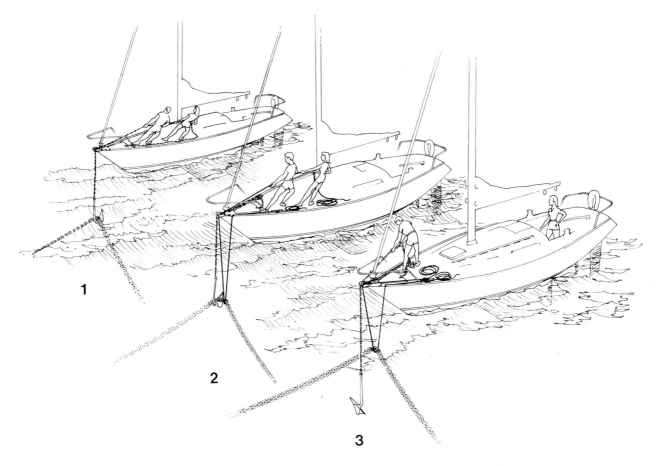

Dealing with a fouled anchor. (1 & 2) Take a line under the offending chain and make it fast at both ends on deck. Work your own anchor free. (3) Retrieve your anchor and let one end of the lifting line g

The most common problem is fouling (snagging) the chain, line or anchor of another boat. Unless you intend to go diving to untangle the mess (not healthy in harbours, or if very short-handed), the only thing for it is to haul both lots up. Assuming, that is, you are not tangled up with the anchor and chain of a mini-liner, in which case it is best to be patient and wait for them to leave. Lifting up an anchor and chain that you have hooked can be hard work and it is best not to be too proud and refuse offers of assistance from well-muscled bystanders, because you don't yet know how big it is. If your cable is all chain, use the anchor winch to get it up. If you don't have one, take a length of line with a running hitch onto the chain and lead it to a cockpit winch.

Once you have brought the offending chain, line or anchor up to the surface, loop a rope under it and back on deck to hold it up. Then let your own anchor down so that the rope takes the weight of the other gear, and work yours free. Once you have retrieved your anchor and cable you can simply release one end of the rope, letting the stranger's tackle go. Don't get your fingers in the way. And don't use a boathook to hold the chain and line, as once you have retrieved your own gear the boathook will be impossible to unhook and will almost certainly go to the bottom with the chain or line.

If you haul up another boat's anchor it is only civil to drop it as far out and in the correct line as possible, so that her crew will not have to re-lay it themselves. With a large anchor over yours and in windy conditions this may be impossible to do and the only thing for it is muttered apologies as you slink out of harbour.

Harbour Practice and Hazards

Although the problems of going stern-to in a crosswind may occupy your mind in harbour, the mechanics of manoeuvring are not the only thing you must watch out for. Lurking inside a harbour are a number of traps that are not always obvious and which you should look out for.

Floating lines Local fishermen throughout the Mediterranean seem to delight in floating, permanent mooring lines that zig-zag all over the place, rarely in orderly lines, and almost certainly across the course you want to take to a berth. The only way to deal with this menace is to nudge your way in slowly, putting the engine into neutral whenever a line looks like getting anywhere near the keel, rudder or propeller. Station someone on the sidedeck with a boathook to try and keep the line away from the boat. Alternatively, find another berth that is not obstructed by a local's mooring line. Whatever you do don't cut the line, even if it should become entangled in the rudder or propeller, or you will find an irate local bearing down on you demanding lots of money.

Local Boats and Sailors Local boats often have macho skippers who like to charge in and out of harbour at full throttle. The bronzed Adonis on the helm will gun his boat out of harbour before throttling down to an economical speed, and likewise will gun her into harbour after pottering back slowly from picking up the nets. Treat local boats with caution when they are coming in and out of harbour and never assume they know the rules of the road. The rule is *you* keep out of the way.

In the case of ferries, it is simply that might is right and again you always keep out of the way. Often they have to perform difficult manoeuvres in a confined space without the aid of a tug, so make sure you give them plenty of room and keep right out of the way.

Local Knowledge In out-of-the-way harbours people are often unfamiliar with the anatomy of a yacht; they don't realise it has bits sticking down into the water or else they don't realise how far rudders and keels extend compared to local boats. Often you will be beckoned into a space by a well-meaning native. When you ask how deep it is, he will roll his eyes and mime that it is deep enough to take a supertanker, and so you will edge in only to run aground. In some instances there will be sufficient depth to get in, but all too often there is not: treat local depths with caution.

In many harbours there are blocks of masonry rubble, old pieces of the quay that fell off some time ago, or chunks of ballast from when it was built, projecting out under water or piled up at the base. Some quays also have a step or ledge below the water level, visible only when you are close in. Care must be taken especially when mooring stern-to, when you can damage the rudder or skeg. Going in bows-first lessens the problem.

Sometimes there may be no quay at all, but just a rough rock breakwater. The only thing to do in this situation is to moor stern-to or bows-to with a long line ashore. Because you will not be able to get the boat close enough to step off you will have to use the dinghy to get ashore. Don't be put off mooring like this or you may miss some utterly charming and idyllic fishing harbours.

Going bows-to can avoid damage in
harbours where rubble slopes down from
the quay.

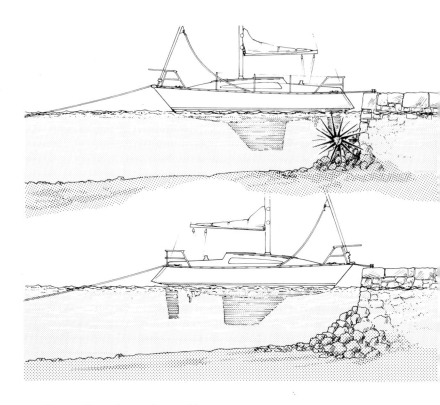

Squeezing in In crowded harbours you are going to have to learn the gentle art of fitting your boat into a space that on first sight appears much too narrow. Only experience will give you an eye for finding a space. See how tightly the boats on either side are spaced and if there appears to be room to push them along a bit you can fit in. Then it is a matter of putting plenty of fenders out and gently nudging your way in. Don't expect the people on the boats on either side of the gap to be entirely happy as you squeeze in and do expect that your idea of the size of the gap can be wrong.

Berthing lines A length of heavy plastic tubing over your lines where they come through the fairleads will cut down on chafe, especially important if the wind and water is moving boats about. A length of tube over the anchor line will cut down on chafe there as well.

Large boats use a length of chain with a carbine clip or similar on the end of a berthing line to cut down on chafe around bollards or rings on the quay. On smaller boats a length of chain on a line thrown ashore is a dangerous item that can seriously injure an innocent bystander. If you feel you need chain on the end of the line put it on afterwards.

Snatching In bad weather with a surge in the harbour you need to prevent the berthing lines snatching as the boat is sucked in and out from the quay. You can buy spring-loaded affairs or more simple rubber gadgets which thread onto the line and take up the tension to ease the snatching load. In extreme conditions, where lines are snapping like cotton thread and deck cleats look like pulling out, a car tyre is the best solution to the problem. Do not tie the ends of the line off to it, but take a couple of turns around either side of the tyre so that the line is continuous from the boat to the quay. Tyres have the advantage of being heavy as well as elastic, so the boat must pull the tyre from the water and then stretch it, thus considerably easing the motion as it surges in and out.

If you are rolling around in a crowded berth and rubbing up against the boats on either side, it is worth pulling yourself out and clear to avoid damage. This is particularly important if boats are rolling, when damage to masts and rigging can occur; adjust lines so that masts and the very vulnerable spreaders do not clash. A squirt of detergent on the fenders will stop them squeaking and disturbing your sleep – if you can sleep, that is.

Other Mooring Techniques

Berthing stern-to or bows-to using your own anchor is far and away the most common method, but in some marinas and harbours there are variations. You still go stern or bows-to, but using a variety of fixed moorings rather than your anchor, as follows.

Posts In some marinas, especially French ones, you must put a line onto a post from your bow or stern and then tie to the quay; the line to the post effectively holds you out instead of an anchor. It is much easier to lead a line around the post and have both ends on the boat rather than attempt to tie the bitter end to the post. This also makes leaving the berth much easier.

Buoyed lines In some marinas you must pick up a buoy which has a line leading to a chain sinker and a mooring block on the bottom. This requires some dexterity with a boathook, especially on boats with high freeboard. Such moorings may not be in good condition: try to provide for this, if possible.

Line tailed to the quay Here the mooring line from the mooring block and sinker is tied at its inner end to the quay. Again dexterity with the boathook is required to pick up the line and lead it to your bow or stern (whichever is *away* from the quay) as quickly as possible. Often a marina attendant will pull the line tight from the quay so you can pick it up more easily. In strong onshore winds it can be difficult to pick up this type of mooring.

Once you are safely berthed it is not a bad idea to ask other boats around you about the strength of the mooring line and chain, and have a good look yourself, especially for corrosion near the surface, or loss of metal where chain links meet. There have been numerous occasions, too many for complacency, where the line or chain has broken in bad weather. In the event of strong onshore winds it is prudent to lay out your own anchor, but place it far enough away to avoid fouling the permanent mooring blocks and chains or you may have to pay for a diver to go down and untangle the mess.

Some small fishing harbours without a quay present problems for berthing, but don't pass them by because of this or you will miss some idyllic spots.

4
Anchoring

There was always something pleasant about doing a thing with competence — even a job as simple as this. As the line came up and down I felt the lead touch and the line slacken.
  'Three fathoms . . . one fathom!'
  Janet cut the engine and we glided in. About twenty yards off the shore she gave the engine a kick astern. The anchor went over with a splash and a rattle of cable. That was one of the moments that I liked best, when the anchor went down in a new harbour, a new island, under a windless sky, with all day to fish or work or read or meet new people.

Ernle Bradford: The Wind off the Islands

Even if you are proficient in the art of anchoring, the Mediterranean presents some special problems, the biggest being the difficult holding ground you will encounter. There will be numerous occasions when you must lay a second anchor to ensure the safety of the boat, and this will often have to be carried out quickly in strong winds and choppy seas. The weather in the Mediterranean can deteriorate with frightening rapidity. Because there are no tides to float you off, should you go aground, your ground tackle may be called upon to extricate you. All in all, you must be familiar with the gear and proficient in the techniques. A lot of it is simply patience and muscle, but a look at the techniques and problems can take the edge off the task.

Anchors

Talking about anchors with someone is like talking about politics or religion. Everyone has their favourites, and whatever I say will be hotly disputed by some and flatly denied by others. I suppose the reason for the volatility of the subject is that the safety of the boat and those on board, not to mention the possibility of a good night's sleep, are dependent on this simple object digging into the sea bottom and holding.

  If you are chartering a boat you will obviously be stuck with whatever gear comes with it. Sadly, this is not always suitable, but an awareness of the limitations of a particular anchor and the chain or rope supplied will help you to make the most of it.

CQR Also known as a plough anchor. It was designed by Sir Geoffrey Taylor who thought that *CQR* would be easier to remember than 'secure'. It has been around for some time now and has the reputation for being the best type of main anchor to have: it has considerable holding power, digs into mud and sand easily, can hook into rock, resets

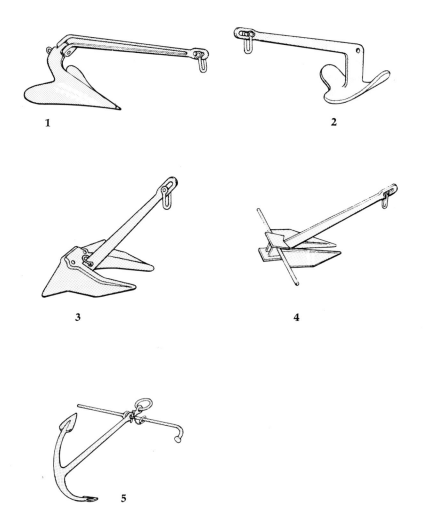

Types of anchor. (1) CQR (2) Bruce (3) Meon (4) Danforth (5) Fisherman.

easily if the pull is exerted in a different direction, and it cannot be fouled by the anchor rode (cable). It is drop-forged so it is a strong anchor, but there have been instances where the pin about which the shank pivots has broken. There is also a problem with imitations, which may be less strongly constructed than the genuine *CQR* which is protected by a patent. The imitations are cheaper, but in the end you pays your money and takes your chances.

The *CQR* is not good at holding in gravel and it can have problems getting through thick weed. According to some of the pundits the sharpness of the point is critical if it is to dig in easily, as is its weight. If the *CQR* does not get through weed it is usually because the point has speared a clump of weed which is preventing it digging in: the anchor must be raised and the weed cleared off it and then you can try again.

Bruce This anchor is a comparatively new type and has been enthusiastically approved by some users and rubbished by others. It was developed for anchoring North Sea oil rigs and only later scaled down for small craft. It is a one-piece drop forged anchor so it is just about indestructable, and there is nothing for the anchor rode to foul. Its shape lets it stow neatly on the bows when pulled up tight to the stemhead. It is good at digging into mud and sand. The difficulty is getting through weed, and it appears that the larger sizes, over 10 kilos, have too large and blunt a blade to cut through it.

Meon Also known as the Brittany or stockless anchor (although there are other stockless anchors). It is not a common anchor but those who use it swear by it. Holding power is good in mud and sand, although not as good as the *CQR* and *Bruce*, and it cuts through weed tolerably well. The disadvantages are its difficult shape for stowing unless the chain comes up through a hawsepipe or it is brought inboard where it will stow flat.

Danforth Although this has great holding power and gets through weed easily, it has two glaring disadvantages. The first is that it is easily fouled by the anchor rode around the stock or the flukes, completely immobilising it. On several occasions I have assisted yachts dragging anchor where the chain has caught around the stock and pulled the anchor out 'backwards'. The second disadvantage is its weak construction: it is welded mild steel and consequently it is easily twisted out of shape or broken by weld failure. As a second anchor or for going stern-to or bows-to it is an excellent choice – its holding power constantly surprises me even with only a small length of chain on and the rest rope.

Fisherman Also called an Admiralty pattern or a Herreshoff. It does not have anything like the holding power of the other anchors, but it will get a grip on almost anything and it gets through weed better than any of the others. It is also useful in very soft mud when the others tend to skate through the top layer and not get down to the firmer stuff. It is not a good main anchor because of the greater weight that must be carried for the same holding effect, and the anchor rode can easily foul the stock or the upper fluke and pull it out. However, some boats prefer to carry it as a main or second anchor where the bottom is known to be exceptionally weedy. Those who do use it swear by it.

Grapnels In many places in the Mediterranean the fishing boats use locally fabricated grapnel anchors. While a few yachtsmen have tried them and say they work well, I have never thought much of them. They do get through weed easily but do not have great holding power; stowage on deck is awkward.

Chain or Rope

The choice between chain or rope or a combination of the two is debated almost as hotly as the choice of anchors. At one time it was advised that the main anchor should be on all-chain cable of sufficient or over-sufficient size for the boat and anchor. It was said in the Mediterranean that you could tell a British boat coming in from the noise of the anchor chain rumbling out and out. Certainly a boat should carry a good length of chain, the actual amount and size depending on her length and displacement. To the end of this, 30 metres of nylon rope can be added for anchoring in moderate to deep depths or for extreme conditions. The advantage of the chain plus rope combination is that when you are anchoring in very deep water there is less weight to haul up but still enough chain hanging in a catenary curve to ensure a horizontal pull on the anchor and to cushion snubbing loads. It also cuts down on weight in the bows where the chain locker is usually placed.

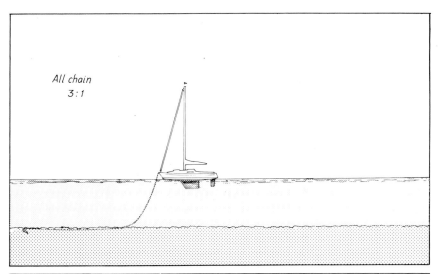

All chain
3:1

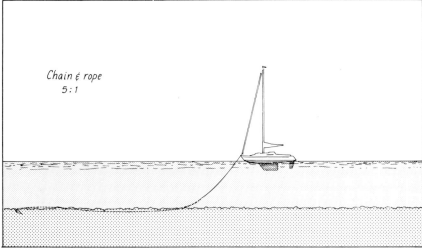

Chain & rope
5:1

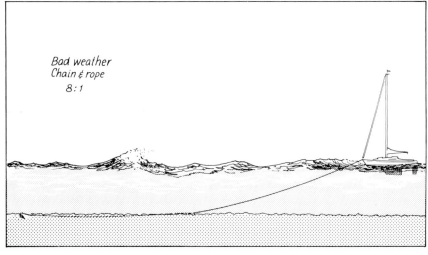

Bad weather
Chain & rope
8:1

Length of the anchor cable in relation to the depth and weather conditions.

As a general rule, in calm weather let go a minimum of three times the depth for all chain, and at least five times the depth for a decent length of chain with rope. In heavy weather you will need to let go at least ten times the depth for a chain and rope combination. Remember to take the height of the bow roller above the water into your calculations for the length of chain and rope to let go: it will usually add at least a metre to the depth of water.

I do not go along with those who argue that much less chain is needed and a greater length of rope can be used because of the superior holding power of modern anchors. In bad holding ground you need the loading on the anchor to be as horizontal as you can get it, especially if you are sheering about the anchor, when it might break out. It will only dig in again if there is chain on the bottom to provide that all-important horizontal pull. Chain on the bottom is also resistant to chafe whereas rope, especially nylon, chafes easily and could wear through on sharp rock. Lastly, a boat on chain or a chain and rope combination will act differently when there are light flukey breezes coming in from different directions. A boat on chain will tend to stay pretty much in the same place, kept there by the weight of the chain, whereas a boat on rope will range about all over the place.

Second and third anchors can be on 5–10 metres of chain with the rest rope. Mostly you will use them as a second anchor in a blow and as the stern anchor when you go bows-to, and you do not require fathoms of chain complicating things. To compensate for the smaller amount of chain use more rope. Longer lengths of chain will get in the way when you are using the anchor off the stern for going bows-to and as you will be doing a lot of this, make it easy for yourself – you will be surprised how well an anchor like the *Danforth* or *Bruce* holds in a straight-line pull even with a short length of chain.

Laying an Anchor

Weed and deep water

There are two problems in anchoring in the Mediterranean that make it a difficult and even irritating task: thick weed on the bottom and the often considerable depths. The biggest problem is weed. The eel-grasses *Zostera marina* and *Cymodocea nodosa*, and Neptune grass, *Posidonia nodosa*, grow prolifically, forming underwater meadows that can be well over a metre thick in places, though usually less. These grasses grow close together and their fibrous roots and branching rhizomes stop an anchor penetrating and digging into the sea bottom. Quite often an anchor will pick up a clump of weed on its point, which clogs it completely. When this happens the only thing to do is haul it up and clear the weed off, otherwise it simply will not set – no matter how much scope you lay out.

The second problem is that you must often anchor in fairly deep water. Many anchorages do not slope gently up to the shore but instead rise abruptly from 10 or 15 metres. For this reason many yachts carry a combination of chain and rope to make anchor handling easier; even some electric anchor winches have difficulty pulling up the combined weight of an anchor and its all-chain cable when it is straight up and down in 15 metres or more. Biceps have even more trouble.

In difficult holding ground with a layer of weed on the bottom, depth also adds to the problem of getting an anchor to dig in and hold properly. There is no easy solution to this: let as much chain and rope out as possible to ensure a semi-horizontal pull on the anchor and keep at it until you are certain it is set well in.

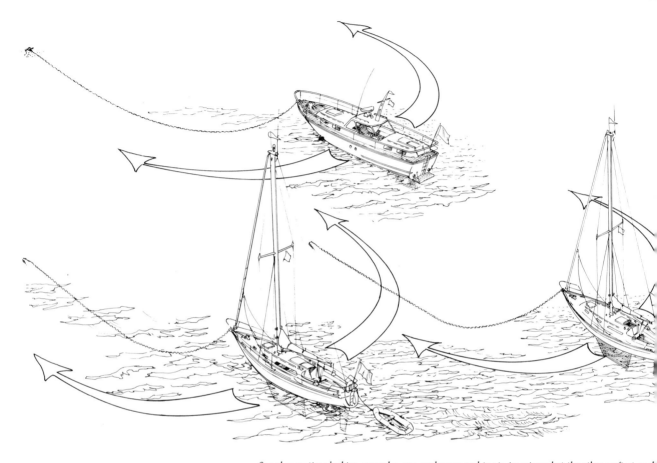

Spend some time looking around a new anchorage and try to imagine what the other craft at anchor will do as they swing. A light motorboat will range about more than a deep keel yacht and consequently take up more 'space' in an anchorage.

With these two problems in mind, spend some time looking around a new anchorage before you decide where to drop the hook. Look carefully at the chart to see if the bottom slopes gently, or suddenly from a hump. Potter around sounding the depths and if you can see the bottom, which is possible even in 10 metres or more, look for a weed-free sandy or muddy patch in which to let down your anchor. See how any other craft in the anchorage are lying and look carefully at the type of boat and its anchoring gear. A heavy deep-draft boat lying to all chain will tend to swing around the chain, which itself acts as an anchor. A light motorboat on rope will range all over the place in the slightest breeze.

While you are checking out the anchorage it is important to have someone experienced up on the bow where visibility is so much better than from the cockpit. They can better assess distances from other boats and rocks or other dangers, and look down into the water. Agreed-upon hand signals will let the person in the bow select a spot with adequate swinging room clear of other boats and to position the anchor over a sandy or muddy patch, free of weed. There is nothing that disturbs an anchorage more than a boat coming in with the skipper and crew arguing and shouting at one another, and nothing so pleasing as a boat that carries out the whole operation in a quiet and seamanlike manner.

slowly astern to dig the anchor in.

Getting the Anchor in

Once the chain and rope has been laid out, go slowly astern until you feel the anchor bite. You can see when it happens by watching the chain or rope, which will come up taut rather than jerking through the water. Once you feel the anchor has taken hold, gradually put the revs up in astern, watching the chain and your position relative to the other boats in the anchorage and the shore to see if the anchor is really holding. Motoring astern like this may sound a little extreme, but if you don't you won't know if it is set or not. It is all too easy for the anchor to hook on a thick clump of weed and appear to be holding only to have the wind change direction or strength and dislodge it – probably when you are ashore with a drink in your hand. With rope you will have to watch more closely to see that it comes up tight and stays so as you are going astern. To double check, while the boat is going astern hold the chain or rope lightly with your hand and you will be able to

Lay the chain and/or rope out along the sea bed rather than dumping it in a pile on the bottom.

feel whether the anchor is bumping over the bottom or holding, via the vibrations travelling up the chain or rope. However do not confuse the chain bumping over the bottom as it straightens out with the anchor dragging: it takes a little experience to be able to feel just what is happening down there.

In some parts of the Mediterranean, in Turkey for example, where you must anchor in deep water on an upward slope, the practice has evolved of taking a line ashore to a tree or rock. The prevailing winds in summer are constantly from the same direction and you will normally be taking the line ashore to 'anchor' the boat against an offshore wind and also to hold the real anchor in place in the uphill-sloping seabed. If you were to swing around the anchor it would be pulled downhill and into deeper water.

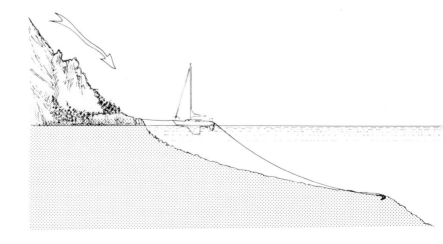

In some parts of the Mediterranean where the sea bottom slopes off steeply the practice has evolved of taking a long line ashore with an anchor off the stern or bows.

ere are rewards for the effort.

This manoeuvre can be done either bows-to or stern-to depending on which is the most convenient for anchoring. If possible put down the main anchor as its chain will help to hold you securely against the wind blowing from a slight angle off the land. In very deep water you will have to make do with the second anchor with a little chain and the rest rope.

When you are anchoring in this fashion, have the dinghy in the water and ready to go with a long line – you will often need 50 or 60 metres – flaked down in the dinghy and the end tied off on the boat. Drop the anchor and go stern or bows-to as close to the shore as possible, then hold the boat in position with the engine while the person in the dinghy rows like fury to the shore. Some care is needed, especially if things start to go wrong, so that the line does not get anywhere near the propeller. If you have a strong swimmer on board it may be possible to swim a line ashore over a *short* distance, but a length of line in the water soon becomes very heavy to tow. Also ensure that the swimmer wears plimsoles to protect his feet from sea urchins and sharp rocks near the shore.

If an anchorage is very crowded or you are in a cove with no swinging room and it is impossible to get a line ashore, you will have to anchor fore-and-aft. Have a look around the spot you are going to occupy and then motor upwind and drop the main anchor. Fall back on this and if necessary tie a length of extra rope to it so you can get back far enough to let the second anchor go over the stern. It is then a matter of adjusting the two until you are happy with the way you are lying and satisfied that both anchors are in and holding.

On occasion you may want to restrict your swinging circle in light flukey winds, but not really go to all the trouble of fore-and-aft anchoring. By dropping the second anchor in a pile over the stern or the bow, its weight will be enough to restrict the swinging circle. Alternatively hang some of the main anchor chain in bights a short distance from the bows. Any heavy weight lowered down the anchor chain will restrict the swinging circle, but do ensure it cannot cause a snarl-up should you need to leave quickly or re-anchor.

Defensive Anchoring in Bad Weather

There always comes a time when you must prepare for the worst. It may be prudent to anchor off rather than tie up to the quay, assuming the port authorities will allow this, or more likely you must anchor defensively in a bay. Although the Mediterranean summer tends to be settled with predictable wind patterns, you can still get small but fierce depressions moving through. In the spring and autumn it is likely you will have a period of unsettled weather – the winter is another matter.

Before you settle down for a blow cast your eye around the other boats at anchor. One of the biggest dangers in an anchorage is that another boat will drag and blow down on yours, creating a disastrous snarl-up. Quite probably the other anchor will foul yours and the two boats will be tied together by their cables and unable to motor up to pick up the anchors. They will be at the mercy of the wind and sea, and may well damage each other. High-sided motor cruisers, and multihulls with a lot of windage and little underneath the water, are bad news in a blow. A deep-keel boat with low topsides on all chain will lie steadily to the wind and will be less likely to break her anchor out, compared to light craft sheering from side to side in the gusts.

Once you have chosen a good spot, lay out the main anchor on all its scope and ensure it is well in. If you know from a pilot book or local knowledge the direction from which the full force of the wind will come, lay a second anchor out at 45° from the main anchor. However, if you are uncertain where the full force of the wind is likely to come from, it may be best to sit on one anchor so that if necessary you can get it up and re-anchor in a better position. You will find that in most cases gusts come from a quadrant depending on the lay of the land around the anchorage, and that some spots will be more sheltered than others.

If you have two anchors out it is best to keep a third anchor ready for instant use should they fail to hold for any reason. If you put the third anchor down, remember there will be no spare should you have to buoy the cables and drop the other two – for instance if another boat drifts down onto you.

Some authorities recommend anchoring in tandem: a second anchor is shackled onto the chain 5–10 metres back from the main anchor. The second anchor then ensures the pull on the main anchor is kept horizontal, and the two anchors work together. It is somewhat complicated to lay and can go wrong. Moreover, if the tandem anchors should drag then you will be short of a second anchor to lay until you have got everything up and sorted things out. As far as I am concerned it is much better to have two separate anchors out on separate lines.

ng a second anchor from the boat. Motor up at an angle of 45° to the main anchor, drop the second
or, and fall back on the two anchors.

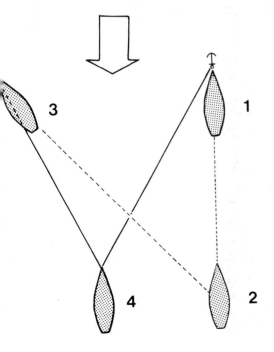

Laying a Second Anchor

The easiest way to lay the second anchor is simply to motor ahead at an angle of 45° to the line of the main anchor and drop it in the desired spot. Before you start, find an object on the shore to line up with when dropping the second anchor, otherwise it is difficult to know exactly where the main anchor is. If the main anchor is on all chain it will not wrap around your keel, rudder or propeller, but will be dragged in a long bight as you motor up. If it is on a chain and rope combination then an eye must be kept on the rope to make sure it doesn't get anywhere near the boat and especially the propeller. Once the second anchor is down, fall back on it and dig it in by going astern. The two anchor cables can then be adjusted to take the strain as the boat sheers across between them.

There may be occasions when you wish to lay out a second anchor from a dinghy. Position the anchor on the back of the dinghy so it can be easily lifted or nudged over the side. The chain should now be flaked in and the rope flaked in after it with the bitter end tied off to the yacht. Have someone on board direct you by pre-arranged hand signals so the anchor can be properly positioned. Now it is a matter of rowing like fury so the rope runs out by itself, pulling the chain which then runs overboard under its own weight and finally snatches the anchor over by itself. If you stop rowing to lay the chain and anchor over the side, the weight of the rope and then the chain will tend to pull the dinghy back to the boat, not to mention the wind pushing you back as well. Use gloves in all of these operations as wet salty rope, chain and heavy anchors are unkind even to calloused hands.

Laying a second anchor from the dinghy. Make life easy for yourself and keep the chain in the dinghy and row out the warp.

Once you have finished and are confident that both anchors are holding, you can sit back with a cup of tea to establish that the boat is not moving. The usual method is to take bearings of objects on the shore and see if these remain more or less the same, making some allowance for sheering around. Other clues are useful. When it is blowing there is a lot of noise as the boat resists the wind and the sea: waves slap and buffet the bows, the mast and rigging shakes and vibrates, and the wind howls and shrieks through the rigging. If the slap of waves on the bows and the shriek of wind in the rigging becomes muted, then there is the possibility you are dragging. Or, with luck, the wind and sea have died down. If the boat lies beam-on to the wind and is not pulled bows into it by the anchor, then she will quite definitely be dragging. The noise a boat makes when buffetted by wind and sea is considerable, and the sudden absence of this noise usually signals that something is wrong. Dragging happens with frightening rapidity, and you must be constantly alert to the behaviour of the boat so that you can take instant action.

As a last resort you may have to stand anchor watches. Whoever is on watch should be properly kitted out for foul conditions, must know how to start the engine and manoeuvre under power, and also where any additional anchoring gear is. And that in the end is all you can do: sit and wait until the wind in the rigging stops shrieking and the sea dies down.

Raising Anchor

Normally a boat is pulled up to her anchor by the crew on the foredeck, by hand or windlass, unless you have an electric anchor winch that does it all. It is important to sit on the foredeck with the feet braced against the pulpit or toerail rather than pull the chain from a standing position or half bent over: the latter is a certain recipe for back trouble. Much can be done to ease this job by gently motoring up to the anchor. If it does not break out of the bottom when the cable is straight up and down, it can be motored out. With the slack pulled in and the remainder straight up and down, and cleated off, motor gently forward and the anchor will be forcibly broken out and can be hauled quickly inboard. Do not rely on holding the line or chain by hand while breaking out: the force is too powerful.

If you do not have an engine or it is not working, an anchor can be sailed out. Since you want to keep the foredeck clear use the mainsail only to tack up to the anchor, shortening up on the cable on each tack and then making fast before the bow swings over. Eventually it will break out on one of the tacks.

An anchor fouled on something on the bottom can be extricated by motoring it out from different angles. Don't apply too much power on the run up as you can easily break the chain with the force of the yacht's weight times her speed. Persistence is the key to this tactic before you try more complicated solutions. If motoring does not work you can take a trip-line down the chain using a chain necklace. Prepare a loop of heavy chain and join the ends around the anchor chain or rope with a shackle to which a line is attached. Lower the necklace down the chain from the dinghy and then try pulling the anchor out from the opposite direction to which it was originally laid.

I don't like using a trip-line to the crown (head) every time one anchors. It complicates laying the anchor, especially in deep water, by getting caught around the chain or rope, and it invariably gets tangled up when you weigh anchor. If the buoy for the trip-line is not properly adjusted to the depth it either lurks just below the surface or floats loose and is easily fouled. A too-short trip-line can hold the anchor off the bottom and prevent it digging in. In practice the anchor is rarely so badly fouled that you need a trip-line, and if you do a necklace can be sent down.

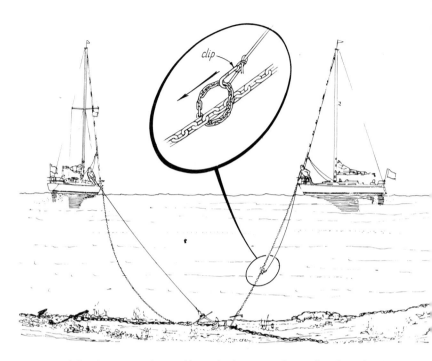

Freeing a fouled anchor using a chain necklace. The object is simply to pull at the anchor from a different direction.

Anchoring Tips

Deck Hardware It is no good having massive anchors and chain if the samson post, cleats or anchor winch cannot take the strains imposed, or even worse aren't securely fastened to the decks with adequate backing pads. If you have doubts about the strength of deck fittings then take the chain or rope to several different fittings in turn. Never leave anchor chain on a winch alone. A friend with a 50 foot steel boat nearly lost it when the bolts holding the electric anchor winch to the deck sheared and the whole lot went over the side taking part of the pulpit with it. Take the strain off a winch with a line or a chain hook made off to a heavy cleat.

Snatching To prevent snubbing take a strong line from the fall of the anchor chain (the part outside the boat and above the water) and lead it back up through a fairlead or the bow roller and make it off on a cleat so it is taking the strain. Nylon line is the best as it is nice and stretchy. The elasticity of the line will not only prevent the chain snatching and jerking the boat uncomfortably as it comes up tight, but will also stop the noise of the chain rumbling over the bow roller. If you are sleeping in the forepeak that can be extremely irritating unless tamed in this way. The anchor cable proper still has to be secured in the normal way: should the 'spring' fail, it takes the strain.

Alarms Many of the new depth sounders have an 'anchor watch' alarm which is useful should the boat drag and move into deeper or shallower water. The alarms are easily set, but some could do with more amplification if they are to wake one from the sleep of the just.

Anchor Lights and Signals International Regulations require all yachts to display a black ball forward when anchored in daylight hours. In the Mediterranean, as elsewhere, this requirement is more honoured in the breach than in fact, by visitors and locals alike. An anchor light should be displayed at night, although in many of the Mediterranean countries, especially in the eastern Med, local boats and many visitors do not. The light will also help you keep an eye on the boat's position when ashore in the evening and also to find it when returning.

Do not assume when you are entering an anchorage at night, that all the boats will be showing an anchor light, because they probably will not. But should you be hit by another boat because you did not have an anchor light, you could be liable for damage to the other boat, and she will have a loophole to wriggle out of paying compensation to you. It will do no good to point out other boats without anchor lights, and in any case you will probably find that they have all miraculously lit up after your accident. Not exhibiting an anchor light may also affect any claims you make for damage, should your insurance company find out.

Lunch Hooks One of the delights of sailing in the Mediterranean is the number of little coves you will come across which although not suitable for an overnight anchorage are suitable for a lunch stop. If your main anchoring gear is heavy and difficult to use you will usually drop your lighter second anchor. Leave someone on board in case the anchor starts to drag. Small boats can anchor by the stern in light conditions, which although it looks silly, directs a welcome breeze into the cockpit and down below.

One of the delights of the Mediterranean is the number of little anchorages you will come across for a lunch stop.

5
Navigation and Pilotage

*Navigation: from the Latin **navis**, a ship, and **ago**, to drive; the art of conducting a vessel from one place on the earth's surface to another by sea safely, expeditiously and efficiently.*

*Pilotage: from the Dutch **peillood**, sounding lead; the act of navigating a vessel coastwise, especially when the land is close aboard and the water shallow.*

The Oxford Companion to the Ships and the Sea: ed. Peter Kemp

Most navigation in the Mediterranean is what can be loosely termed coastal navigation. The reason for this is very simple: the Mediterranean is an almost land-locked sea with many headlands and larger masses of land jutting into it together with a large number of islands. The ancients would navigate from island to island and around the coasts, picking up local pilots. To a large extent navigation for the modern yachtsman consists of island-hopping or coasting, within sight of land or a short distance away from it. There are few really long open water passages to be made and for the most part these can be avoided by sailing along a coast or to an island a short distance away. The Mediterranean navigator comes to rely on his dead reckoning and what can loosely be termed eyeball navigation. This chapter is mostly addressed to the latter, a nebulous subject that hovers somewhere between coastal navigation and pilotage. Allied to basic, careful coastal navigation, it will enable you to get around the Mediterranean safely and enjoyably.

Eyeball Navigation: a primer

Coastal navigation consists of establishing your position in relation to a visible coastline and any invisible, underwater hazards. Charted landmarks such as mountain peaks and capes, lighthouses and buoys, are chosen and by taking fixes on these, the boat's position is established and marked on the chart. With the new breed of electronic position finding equipment the task of finding a boat's position can be further simplified. Given all this, why is it that the work of establishing a position on a chart is so often fraught with worry and doubt? Previous experience will do much to alleviate such uncertainty, but you can also make things much easier by thoroughly preparing for the task.

Preparation

When you approach a familiar coastline or enter a harbour you have been to several times, you feel confident about it. From previously navigating along the coast you have a

Most navigation in the Mediterranean is coastal navigation of the sort where eye-balling the coast and identifying features along it gets you around.

mental picture and the experience to recognise the prominent features that show where you are: mountain peaks, ridges, capes, rocky bluffs, villages and towns, lighthouses. In entering a familiar harbour you know where the dangers lie, where the safe channel is and where the shoal water lies, the best place to anchor or berth, and where the wind will blow from. Already having such a chunk of diverse information allows you to pilot your boat with confidence while you assess the present conditions of sea and wind for other potential dangers. It is acquiring this sense of familiarity in unfamiliar waters that eyeball navigation is all about.

Before you encounter an unfamiliar stretch of coast or a new harbour you must prepare for it as thoroughly as possible by swotting up on the charts and pilot book covering the area. The two-dimensional aerial view of a chart must be converted to what you imagine will be the three-dimensional view you see from low down in a boat. It is an art that comes only with practice. On the chart, look at the contours of the land, at mountain peaks, cliffs, vegetation or the lack of it, roads which often leave conspicuous scars on steep-to land, the buildings close to the water and farther inland, the capes and headlands and whether they end abruptly or slope gently down to sea level, the islands and rocks around the coast, and imagine how all these features will fit into a three-dimensional view from near sea level. Some will be obscured, other features will increase in prominence or distinctiveness against their backgrounds. On older charts features such as vegetation, roads and villages must be used with caution since they may well have disappeared or changed radically since the original survey. Sadly many of the new metric charts omit valuable detail on and inland from the coast.

Use a pilot book to flesh out this picture, although if you are using an Admiralty Pilot remember it was written with ships in mind and that there is a mass of information in the carefully mannered style of the Hydrographer that is of little concern for the small-craft navigator. Yachtsman's pilots give more inshore detail as well as much information that would be irrelevant for ships. Use approach sketches and photographs but treat them with some caution. Many of the Admiralty drawings were made in the last century and while they give a useful idea of the topography do not trust the details of buildings and vegetation depicted. Photographs of approaches can be misleading and don't seem to have the timeless quality of the Admiralty sketches. In areas where tourism has increased in the last few years, a single new apartment block or hotel built after the photograph was taken can confuse the image given.

Depending on where it is viewed from, a headland or mountain will take on different shapes. The Admiralty recognised just how different the same mountain peak or cape could look from different angles, and often gives two or more sketches showing the same feature from two different angles. It is all too easy to assume you are coming up to a prominent headland when in fact you are looking at a coastal bulge before the headland you want. Study the chart for such possible confusions and identify lighthouses or other unmistakable buildings that can eliminate it.

Once you have mulled over the chart and pilot, jot down a few brief notes. These are to jog your memory and not to replace the mental picture you have built up. What you are trying to achieve is a familiarity with the coast or anchorage before you have seen it. Once you have built up a mental map, pick out the dangers shown on the chart: a reef, isolated underwater rocks, a rock just above water, a shallow wreck, shoal water. Plot clearing bearings or transit bearings to avoid them. The art here is not so much to determine where you are as to know where you are not: you might be anywhere within say a square mile of sea, quite safely, so long as you know you are not where the danger lies. One way to stay clear of a danger is to use a clearing bearing.

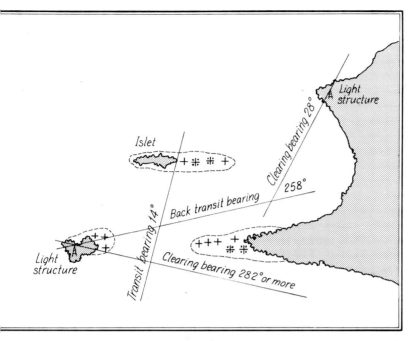

Deadman's Reef Passage: Using transit and clearing bearings to find your way through a reef passage. In practice you use the bearings as an aid to visually picking your way through the reef passage.

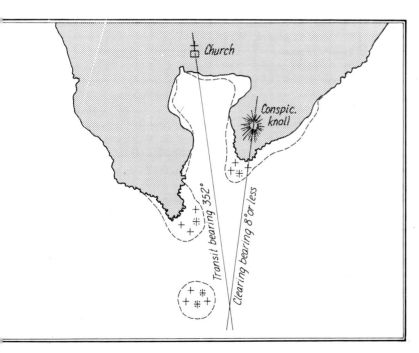

Solace Bay: Getting safely into an anchorage using clearing and transit bearings. The water over the reefs will show up as different colours – different shades of blue, green and brown. Use Polaroid sunglasses which accentuate the different colours.

When using a transit bearing, a line between two fixed objects, you follow a course between dangers, in the safe water. Choose charted objects unlikely to have changed: the tip of a cape, a peak, a rocky bluff, a small island or a rock above water; and man-made objects unlikely to have been destroyed or obscured such as a lighthouse, a castle, an isolated church spire or tower. Avoid using a tree described as 'conspicuous', or a house or a hotel. The tree may have been chopped down or others grown up, the house may have been demolished or others built, and one hotel looks much like another in this age of unfortunate architecture. Clearing and transit bearings should be plotted on your chart and then jotted down with your brief notes. Once you have developed the technique of swotting up a coast or anchorage, you will find your notes contain little more than conspicuous landmarks, clearing and transit bearings, and the depth you will anchor or berth in.

Build into all of this escape routes in case the weather should deteriorate. Imagine your engine is out of action and work out where you can safely sail to. In case the wind shifts or blows up, research what alternative harbours and anchorages you can use. Not only will this save looking over the chart and thumbing through the pilot book in a panic, but it gives you a breathing space to snug down the boat and prepare for whatever is coming. Knowing the alternatives is necessary if your chosen harbour becomes untenable for any reason. The thoroughly aware yachtsman is not only equipped to revise his plans but is then more relaxed about his sailing as a whole.

In Practice

By having a mental picture of a place, you can pilot a boat in without constantly looking at the chart and pilot. You will be able to search out dangers, confirm landmarks, work out what has changed, and keep an eye on other boats in the vicinity and on your progress in relation to all this. Always doubt that you know exactly where you are, and keep checking your position to make sure you are nowhere near potential dangers. Use the humble hand bearing compass to identify marks and produce a cocked hat with your boat somewhere in it. When negotiating a channel keep the echosounder on, and if it has a shallow depth alarm set it for the depths along the edges of the fairway.

Above all, master the art of making your boat go slowly. In the final stages of your approach to an unfamiliar destination give yourself breathing space should things not turn out quite as you anticipated. In the Mediterranean this is so much easier to do as there are no tidal streams to whisk you away if you hold back or stop. It is very exciting to rush into a narrow bay but it may not turn out to be the one you thought it was, it's better to check and re-check.

In an anchorage or harbour, a mental map of the place and a few predetermined clearing and transit bearings leave you time to look around for possible dangers: a gust coming across the water which might catch you out, the sea ruckling over shallow water, other boats anchoring or manoeuvring, ferry berths and approaches, odd buoys and fishing floats – and where, oh where, are you going to moor. You are 'free' to appraise all these things with occasional reference to the pilot and chart without a mad panic ensuing as you glance from the pilot and chart to the anchorage and back again, not knowing where you are or where you are going. With a little preparation a glance at the chart will jolt your memory and renew and confirm your mental map. Furthermore, you're then in a better position to turn and go back out if anything seems wrong. It's a good idea to put your chart and pilot open at the right page into a clear plastic case so that spray can't damage them and weight the lot down on the cockpit seat so that the wind can't blow them away.

...neone should be up front to con you into an anchorage or harbour using an agreed system of hand ...nals.

When piloting through a tricky passage with rocks or shoal water on either side, or into a difficult anchorage or harbour, put someone up in the bows to keep a lookout and con the way in. From the bows or on top of the cabin by the mast, he can get an uncluttered view of possible dangers and of the clear way ahead. Arrange a simple code of signals beforehand. Do everything at low speed and if in doubt use the engine to just maintain position while you sort out where you are and where the dangers lie. When you are looking for an isolated rock or buoy, or the greeny-brown water over a reef or shoal, search all around for it and don't look only where you think it should be. It will often appear where you least expect it.

Binoculars can be most useful, particularly if your long-distance vision is not all that it might be, or used to be. For twilight work, because of their light-gathering powers they make a great difference. One almost essential piece of equipment is a pair of Polaroid sunglasses. Polaroids cut out glare off the water surface and thus help you see down into the water, and accentuate the colour differences over different depths. Reefs and shoal water show up as green and brown patches which are otherwise all but impossible to see with the naked eye; they do not show up as well with non-Polaroid sunglasses.

At night you must identify all lights with absolute certainty. Study the chart and harbour plan carefully for any possible confusion of lights. In some harbours where there is an outer and inner basin, one of the lights at the entrance of the inner basin could be mistaken for an outer entrance light. In the Mediterranean the characteristics of lights are not always different for an inner and outer basin or breakwater. Inside a harbour or anchorage I don't like to use a searchlight or powerful torch until the last moment: it gives a limited field of view and blots out the overall picture. Let your eyes adjust to the dark, look around slowly, and you will be surprised what you can pick out. Most Mediterranean nights are clear and if there is no moon the stars provide enough light to pick things out. On nights when there is a full moon there is almost enough light to read by. Use your ears to pick up clues as well: keep the crew quiet and listen for waves breaking, water lapping, a jangling halyard or rumbling chain from a boat at anchor. Close in, you can use a light to examine the quay or pinpoint a boat at anchor, but it will destroy your nightsight for several minutes.

Before you drop anchor or moor, spend some time sizing things up and assessing the various options open to you. If other boats are at anchor or berthed watch how they are lying to the wind and sea and look around for dangers that might cause problems. Are there gusts making anchoring or berthing difficult? Is there rock ballast along the quay making it difficult to get a line ashore? Are there laid moorings which might foul your anchor, or floating mooring lines that might get caught around the propeller? Where will you end up if the anchor drags and what will happen if the wind turns around in the night? If you can't see things clearly send someone to scout around in the dinghy while you potter about a safe distance off.

Mastering eyeball navigation will not only help you bring your boat safely along the coast and into harbour, it will also enhance your pleasure in new landfalls and new harbours. You will have time to look around and enjoy where you are going, to smell and listen to the place, to feel a sense of delight and achievement at arriving comfortably and competently.

Navigation and Piloting Hazards

In many ways navigation and pilotage in the Mediterranean is easier than in the tidal waters of the English Channel or the current and reef-strewn waters of the Pacific. The virtual absence of tides removes at a stroke a signifcant factor that complicates navigation in most other parts of the world. The clarity of the water makes spotting reefs and shoal water very much easier. Despite this there are hazards which if not peculiar to the Mediterranean are something to be especially aware of.

Haze In the summer a heat haze often lies over the coast and islands reducing visibility considerably, sometimes to a mile or less but normally to two to three miles. Often you will be sailing along looking for the coast when suddenly it will appear like a mirage sitting on the water. A faint line of a mountain peak or ridge will appear to be followed by a faint shoreline that hardens and resolves itself into features you at last recognise. The haze is composed of fine dust and water vapour, and although you would think a fresh breeze would dispel it, it will not. Heavy rain cleanses the air leaving the seascape brilliantly clear, so much so that it looks dramatically different with the true distances telescoped compared to apparent distances in the haze.

Sea Mist Parts of the Mediterranean – Turkey, the Ionian Sea and Cyprus in particular, experience a dense radiation fog on summer mornings which can reduce visibility to a quarter of a mile. The mist usually disperses by the afternoon, but I have known it to last all day and to extend several miles to seaward. In such conditions coastal navigation becomes rather more demanding. In the winter fog occurs occasionally in the northern Mediterranean but rarely on the southern side.

Reefs and Rocks Compared to the Atlantic or Pacific, the Mediterranean is a shallow sea. The deepest part, the Matapan Trench in the Ionian Sea, drops to a depth of 4400 metres, only slightly greater than the average depth of the Atlantic and a trifle beside the 11,022 metres of the Marianas Trench in the Pacific. Paradoxically, for yachtsmen one of its attractions is the considerable depth right up close to the shore; most of the coast and islands drop steeply into the sea and the absence of any real tide means you can sail close to the land and sight-see.

...oking down over the anchorage at Kekova in Turkey where the reefs at the entrance show up well as ...erent coloured patches of water.

Conversely, as well as the land dropping sheer into the sea, it also juts up abruptly. Rocks and reefs project straight up from the sea bottom, often from considerable depths; it is not unusual for a rock to be surrounded by 40–50 metres of water, presenting an isolated danger. Because many of the charts for the Mediterranean were surveyed in the last century they are not as accurate as might be desired and a rock or reef may not be at exactly the latitude and longitude indicated.

This combination of a peculiar marine topography and sometimes inaccurate hydrography means that you should treat marked rocks, reefs, shoal water, and tapering headlands that might extend out underwater, with some respect. Give them a wide berth rather than cutting corners: not everything is steep-to. In a fresh breeze the disturbed water over a rock or reef cannot be distinguished from the whitecaps whipped up by the wind. And with deep water all around a depthsounder is little use – you will be on the reef before it can tell you anything other than what you already know, that you're stuck or holed. A boat moving at speed, especially a power boat, will usually rip her bottom open on one of these marine can-openers and go straight down on the other side.

Currents Although the Mediterranean has virtually no tides, there are other factors which cause currents. Water pours in through the Straits of Gibraltar to replace that which evaporated, and circulates around the Mediterranean in a roughly anti-clockwise direction. However, because numerous lumps of mainland and islands obstruct this flow the currents are difficult to predict, and winds contrary to the current can hold up or even reverse it. In most cases a guestimate must be made for the effect of current on your dead reckoning, based on the predicted currents and the strength and direction of the wind over the last week or so. Allow for the *possibility* of a current, if in doubt.

Fishing Nets In some parts of the Mediterranean long surface nets are laid some distance out at sea, to catch swordfish and tunny. The old style nets, called variously *mattanza*, *madragues* and *tonnara*, permanently anchored along the migration routes of the fish off parts of southern Italy, Sicily, Sardinia, Tunisia, France, and Spain, are now rarely laid: too much labour is involved for diminishing catches. But the buoyed surface nets laid from fishing boats are used extensively around Sicily, the Lipari Islands and off the western Italian coast up to Salerno, and sometimes in Spanish waters. The wide mesh nets can be up to 3 kilometres long and are laid in a giant zig-zag pattern at around 2200 HRS and hauled in again around 0300 to 0600 HRS. They are often poorly lit, and if you get caught up in one the best thing to do is to take the sails down and wait until the nets are gathered in. Usually the mother fishing boat will spot you and direct you around the end of the net. Sometimes the ends are marked by small open boats.

Other fishing methods practised in the Mediterranean are less of a problem. Most nets hung between buoys are weighted bottom nets, and most buoyed long-lines and pots do not have trailing lines to get caught up in. Sometimes a fishing boat will tie a long line to the shore and attach a net to this to encircle an area. Keep your eyes peeled when you see fishing buoys and flags as fishermen are endlessly ingenious at dreaming up ways of leaving lines and nets so they will catch around propellers and skegs. At night small boats use powerful lamps to attract fish and as the boat rides to the swell the bobbing light can be mistaken for a navigation aid. Such lamps obscure the vessel's coloured nav lights because of their intensity, and of course ruin the fishermen's own night vision so that they are unlikely to spot a dimly lit yacht. This can also be true of larger vessels such as trawlers.

Magnetic Variation Throughout the Mediterranean variation is mostly less than 3° and in many places it is 1° or less with a slow annual increase. At Gibraltar it is 5° W, but at Ibiza it is just over 3° W and in the eastern Mediterranean it is 1°50'. In practice it is rarely worth bothering about on very short trips as it is difficult to steer a small boat within an accuracy of 3°, but on any longer passages it is worthwhile making the correction.

Buoyage In most of the Mediterranean the IALA 'A' Maritime Buoyage System has now been introduced and it is currently being implemented in the eastern Mediterranean, although the schedule for completion in Turkey and eastern North Africa is unknown. That, you might think, is the end of the story, but unfortunately it is not. Buoyage exists for the most part only around large commercial ports and along the commercial shipping routes. Away from the large ports and shipping routes do not expect to find a systematic buoyage system: indeed do not expect to find buoys at all in some places. Many narrow channels and dangers to navigation are not buoyed or marked and this is why eyeball navigation becomes an all-important art to acquire.

Lights Much the same applies to lights as to buoyage. On the whole the Mediterranean is fairly well lit, but there is so much land sticking into the sea and so many islands and rocks jutting up into it that it would be nearly impossible to put lights everywhere. Some countries are not as good at maintaining lights as others, so exercise caution and do not assume that because you cannot see a light, it is not there. Off the Turkish coast I have been 'lost' when sailing at night only to discover later that a major light was not working.

A further complicating factor is the reduction in the effective range of lights in the Mediterranean. The formula for calculating the candlepower of a light has a figure for atmospheric transmissivity built into it, and this figure is decreasing worldwide as the developed world releases all sorts of pollution into the air. You should reduce the range of the lights in the Mediterranean by around 10–12% if you are not using up-to-date charts or a recent Admiralty List of Lights.

Navigation Equipment

In the age of the omnipotent microchip it seems as if all problems of navigation and piloting are reduced to choosing from the array of electronic goodies in the glossy pages of the yachting magazines. It is all too easy to get this impression when faced with the choice and sophistication of the new electronic navigation aids on the market: position-finding at the touch of a button by Satnav, Decca, Loran, Omega or a combination of aids interfaced to reduce error; radar large and small with computer enhanced images and colour display; on-board computers that integrate direction, speed, distance run, tidal streams and currents and whatever you can feed into them to give constantly updated DR positions. The age of electronic navigation is here and the joke about an automatic yacht free of human error is a possibility. Or is it?

It is easy to forget that these electronic black boxes are *aids* to navigation and not a replacement for the art of safely navigating a vessel. Computer folk know full well that the equipment does not think, it processes information – 'rubbish in, rubbish out' is the maxim. The same criterion should be adopted by the thinking navigator surrounded by digital readouts, because any rubbish or faulty information fed in by hand on the instruments recording data (and that can be as simple as a log with weed on the impeller or spinner) will result in faulty output. Before the advent of the new electronic wizardry, position-finding was by dead reckoning and celestial navigation. The instruments used and practice in handling his sextant give the navigator a sense of accuracy and error, a feel for the reliability of readings and sights that can be checked by eye or by taking more sights. You are in tune with the measuring process and the working of results. To a great extent this is also true of radio direction-finding: practice is important.

The two-dimensional view of a chart must be converted to what you imagine will be the three-dimensional view you see from a boat.

The greatest loss occurring with the advent of the newer electronic navigation aids is the loss of the art of eyeball navigation. Once you can see and identify features on the land, no amount of electronic accuracy can substitute for placing your boat's position on a chart in relation to what you see with the two God-given instruments placed just below your forehead. They can navigate your boat through a narrow passage fringed by reefs in a way no computer can. You can hone eyeball navigation to a fine art that no amount of microchip technology can imitate, and take your boat into places where no digital readouts can. Electronic wizardry helps but cannot replace that most marvellous of on-board computers between your ears – yet.

In the Mediterranean you can safely navigate a yacht, as many do, with the minimum of equipment: steering compass, hand bearing compass, log and depth sounder. Before you splash out on expensive equipment make sure you don't skimp on the quality of basic equipment, including charts and pilots for the areas you will be in. Much of your navigation will be of the eyeball variety, indeed it must often be so. Accurate position-finding equipment like Satnav or Loran is useful, especially on long passages, but for the reasons outlined below, it can also get you into trouble. In the end, one still has to be able to rely on one's compass and dead reckoning skills.

Radio Direction Finders The humble RDF has become less fashionable in the last few years, but it is still a cheap and useful tool for navigation in the Mediterranean where there are plenty of radio beacons with good ranges. There are some grouped marine radio beacons, but most are aero beacons which can be used with the relevant cautions. RDF is useful for homing in on and giving you a rough position check away from the coast. Approaching the two low-lying islands of Malta early one winter, I kept losing sight of them as thunderstorms passed over blotting out everything with torrential rain and reducing visibility to half a mile or less. There are two strong radio beacons on Malta and I used these to home in on the islands until I could see them. There are radio beacons dotted all around the Mediterranean that can be used in this way and they provide an effective aid to navigation that is a very cheap form of electronics.

Satnav This type of position-finding equipment is by now justifiably popular on cruising boats, providing accurate fixes at a fairly low price. Though the Transit satellites are scheduled to shut down in 1994, it is difficult to see how the Americans will be able to do this without undermining public confidence in their satellite systems. The likelihood is that the system will go on operating into the next century until its replacement, the Global Positioning System, popularly known as Navstar, is fully in commission and the numbers of civilian receivers outnumber those for Satnav. In the Mediterranean there are just as many satellite passes as elsewhere, around one every 108 minutes, which gives a theoretical average of 0.05 miles accuracy. In practice, when a yacht is underway Satnav will produce fixes with an accuracy of around a quarter of a mile, assuming accurate boat speed and heading inputs. However, if the latter are inaccurate, then the accuracy of the fix decreases.

Decca Navigator The introduction of cheaper small-craft Decca receivers with the facility to give position directly in latitude and longitude rather than Decca co-ordinates has boosted the system's popularity. While coverage in North European waters is good, the coverage in the Mediterranean extends over only a part of Spain and Morocco at present.

Loran C The wisdom of buying Loran is limited by the cost of a receiver and the question mark hanging over its future after the USA introduces GPS/Navstar. Like Satnav it is likely that the transmitters will continue to operate into the next century, even though the official line is that the present contract requires the transmitters to be open only until 1992.

In the Mediterranean, the master station transmits from Cantanzaro in Italy with slave stations on Lampedusa Island in Italy, Kargaburun in Turkey and Estartit in Spain. Reliable reception is stated to be around 1000 miles, but a realistic accuracy would be about half this distance from the transmitter. This means that the accuracy of the system is reduced at either end of the Mediterranean. At a distance of 1500 miles from the transmitter the accuracy of Loran can be as poor as 10 miles. All in all, the accuracy of Loran does not match that of Satnav, and its cost probably means that most people would consider buying an alternative.

Global Positioning System/Navstar This second generation satellite system is the one that will eventually take over; Satnav and Loran will become redundant with the greater accuracy of this system, expected to be to 20 metres for military users and 100 metres for civilian sets. Navstar is intended to be fully operational in the early '90s, and depending on cost the civilian version is likely to become the most popular long-range system. However, there may well be delays, and all complex systems and their equipment require time for de-bugging and for prices to fall.

The Problems of Accuracy

The paradox of the more sophisticated position-finding equipment is that you end up with a position on the earth which is more accurate than the charts you are plotting it on. Many of the charts for the Mediterranean and other parts of the world were surveyed in the late 19th century using astronomical sights and other methods and have not been much improved since. Some, but not all, of these charts carry a warning, and corrections for latitude and longitude that can be more than 1 mile. So we end up in the anomalous position of knowing where we are in terms of latitude and longitude to within say 100 metres but having a chart to find out where we are in relation to the land or the sea bed with an accuracy of perhaps less than a mile. Blind acceptance of the position given by say Satnav or Loran can lead to disaster, because the actual position of a danger or the land is not exactly where it is shown on the chart.

The problem is further compounded when the equipment you are using gives no or little indication of the degree of accuracy with which any particular fix has been computed. It all happens invisibly, purring chips processing information quickly and silently until the final figures are produced. In bad weather or bad visibility any of us will grab at the magic result without knowing what sort of accuracy it represents. The only defence is to respect and maintain your compass, log and RDF, keep dead reckoning up to date, and cross-check fixes by other means whenever possible.

In the future it is likely that new charts, quite possibly surveyed by satellites and stored digitally, will be produced; but who is to make them and correct them, and who will pay for them is a problem yet to be solved. And what would happen should all this information be accidentally erased? Recently, a yacht passing the massive transmitting and monitoring station on the eastern end of Cyprus found that all its instruments had failed. Once past the station they began to function again but all the information stored in memory was lost. There is something solid and reassuring about paper and ink.

These accurate position-finding aids are a welcome addition for passage-making, but close to the coast or any dangers to navigation they must be used prudently. Eyeball navigation rules when you are coasting, or entering a harbour or anchorage.

Radar

This tends to be looked upon as primarily a collision avoidance device rather than as an aid to navigation in yachts. Its virtues lie in its ability to produce an accurate picture of what is there (or rather, what will return the radar beam), and it is especially valuable in bad visibility and at night. The latter is particularly useful along badly lit stretches of coast where it might otherwise be perilous to proceed. The introduction of smaller and lighter scanners and screens with computer enhanced images, and all this at a cheaper price, has brought radar out of the big-yacht bracket and into smaller boats. If you are going to do extensive coastal cruising, think long and hard on the virtues of radar over electronic position-finding equipment if you have to make a choice between the two.

Amps and Gremlins

All electronic equipment eats up current and you may need to upgrade your battery and charging equipment to produce enough power. The average working consumption of instruments needs consideration and when combined with the power needed for your instruments and black boxes, plus lighting and all the other amp-gobbling electrical equipment on board, you may well find that you are using more than you can supply. To have to run your engine to be able to use the radar, as one sailing boat needed to do, seems rather a travesty of the idea of sailing. Fitting an extra battery, a more powerful alternator or a generator will supply the amps you need, but the cost cannot be overlooked.

Apart from supplying sufficient power, you should consider what may happen when electronics malfunction. Facilities for the care and repair of such equipment, especially the more complicated devices, are few and far between in the Mediterranean. In the eastern Med and North Africa you will be hard pushed to find reliable electronic repair facilities, although the local radio and television repair shops will 'have a go'. If they do, your warranty will almost certainly be invalidated. Despite the fact that some manufacturers list certified repair agents in a number of countries, the best policy is to return the instrument to the factory. The delay, cost and trouble of getting it back and dealing with Customs may be considerable, though.

e-balling into a harbour. Shallow water fringes this channel into Poros in Greece.

And if you are choosing

After updating, and if you are cautious duplicating, some of your basic equipment and buying a full set of charts and pilots, you may be considering what to buy in the way of position-finding equipment. For Mediterranean use, the requirements are different from those needed if crossing an ocean since you will inevitably be relatively close to land rather than somewhere in a watery expanse.

First choice must be an RDF set, since it is now comparatively cheap to buy quite sophisticated equipment. Radio beacons are well established and cheap to maintain and operate, so it is likely they will continue to operate for some time yet. Installation cost is very reasonable, and it usually incorporates a radio receiver.

Second choice would be the current form of Satnav, since GPS/Navstar is not yet in commission and its receivers are initially going to be expensive. When it becomes fully operational and the cost comparable to Satnav, then it should become the logical choice.

Third choice must be for radar, and as I have already indicated, it jostles Satnav for priority. Reliable and intelligently interpreted radar can greatly aid coastal navigation by providing an accurate map and an accurate position, thus avoiding the problems of position-finding equipment vis-a-vis less accurate charts.

6
Staying Healthy

'Sea-voyages have a powerful curative effect on some invalids, but they do not generally bring healthy persons into very good condition. If it is calm, landsmen over-eat themselves, take too little exercise, sleep badly, and get their bowels constipated. If it is rough, they suffer from sea-sickness and the badness of ventilation below.'

T.K. Chambers: *A Manual of Diet in Health and Disease, 1876*

You are setting off on the trip of a lifetime, so it makes sense to take as much care as possible of your health; to guard against major ills and to watch out for minor ones such as sunburn or an upset tummy that could otherwise spoil your sojourn in the Mediterranean. Falling ill abroad will not only mar your stay but can cost you a hefty sum of money if you are not properly insured. Ignore making arrangements and you put not only your health at risk but your wallet as well. The following is a brief guide to the preparations you should make before you travel, and remedies for common ailments found in the Mediterranean. However, it is stressed that all this should be talked over with your doctor, particularly if you have any special medical problems. I'm not a doctor.

Before you go

Treatment within the EEC
Travellers from EEC countries can get urgent treatment free or at reduced cost if on a temporary visit to another EEC country. Check before you go regarding your status in this matter, to make sure you are eligible: the self-employed and unemployed may not be; it depends on previous employment status. Once you have establshed that you are eligible, get leaflet SA30, *Medical Costs Abroad*, from your local Department of Health and Social Security office. In the centre of the leaflet you will find Form CM1: fill it in and send it off not more than six months before you leave. The DHSS will send you form E111 which you must carry with you and present if you need treatment abroad. If this all sounds complicated, don't worry because in practice it is easily carried out if you have complied with all the prerequisites.

In some countries you will receive only a part of your treatment free, commonly 70 per cent, and in most countries you must first pay the fees in full after treatment and then claim it back in that country. This can be a complicated procedure, and the part treatment

You are setting off on the trip of a lifetime, so it makes sense to take as much care as possible of your health. This yacht has a canvas wind scoop over her fore-hatch.

you pay for out of your own pocket can cost a lot, particularly if you needed specialist attention or extensive diagnostic tests. For this reason it is worthwhile taking out medical insurance for the period you are away; and at the very least, cover for any additional payments made for treatment over and above that agreed between the EEC countries. The EEC agreement does not cover pre-existing conditions such as high blood pressure or diabetes, and nor will it always cover treatment related to pregnancy, abortion or nervous disorders, dentistry or cosmetic surgery. If you are living and working in another EEC country the reciprocal agreement does not apply and private cover should be taken out. Two countries in the Mediterranean, Malta and Yugoslavia, have an agreement with the United Kingdom to give free or reduced cost treatment for urgent cases.

Medical Insurance

Assuming you are not at death's door, medical insurance can be obtained at very reasonable rates from a number of large insurance companies, sold through airlines, tour operators, travel agents and banks. Thomas Cook, for example, offers cover from 'Europ Assistance', a large and reliable insurance company specialising in travel and medical insurance. Tour operators running sailing holidays make insurance compulsory on booking a holiday, but you must check that there is adequate cover for medical expenses including sufficient funds to fly you home should you need specialist care not available in that country. Always read the small print carefully to discover exactly what you are covered for, and more important, what the exclusions are. You may find that, apart from specified pre-existing health conditions, you are not covered for accidents while skindiving, on mopeds, water skiing, other water sports or sailing races. Small companies running sailing holidays will not always offer adequate cover for medical treatment and if this is the case find your own cover from another source. It is worth shopping around, for both terms and prices vary widely: try airlines' policies and look out for any sailing exclusions.

Travellers with their own private medical insurance or from countries with private health care, and in particular American travellers, should check whether their insurance policy covers them for full medical diagnosis and treatment abroad. In the United Kingdom, both BUPA and PPP give only limited cover abroad. The American Blue Cross and Blue Shield plans give limited cover abroad, and the Medicare plan gives none. In most cases it is wise to take out additional travel insurance so you are not caught out.

Apart from your medical insurance documents, carry a card in your wallet, or better still wear a bracelet or dog-tag, with any vital personal medical information on it: blood group, drug and food allergies, insulin dosage for diabetics, and so on. If you have any existing medical problems, a heart condition or high blood pressure for instance, carry a doctor's letter setting out these problems and the treatment you have been receiving for them, including any special medication. Try to have any mention of drugs in both generic as well as trade names: this can simplify obtaining the right preparation or informing a strange doctor.

Precautions before you go

It is not obligatory at present to be immunized against anything before you are permitted to enter any of the countries around the Mediterranean, but this does not mean you should not take some precautions. Your own doctor should be able to advise you which vaccinations you may need while on holiday or living in the Mediterranean. The School of Hygiene and Tropical Medicine in London runs a service which, for a fee, advises on problems of health and prevention overseas and provides innoculations; it is open to the public, without referral from another doctor. British Airways and some other airlines and tour operators can also advise.

If you are going to spend some time in the Mediterranean, it is wise to be protected against polio and also to have a combined typhoid and tetanus (TABT) course of injections (two injections a month apart). The tetanus part of the vaccination is important should you pick up any nasties when hauling up the anchor from a dirty harbour, especially if the chain is rusty or you have a fresh wound on the hand. In many of the countries around the Mediterranean it can be difficult to get a tetanus jab if you are injured. In Rhodes, after I had cut my toe badly, I hobbled up to the hospital where the doctor told me to go into town and get the vaccine from the chemist and then return for him to administer it. I guess I was lucky there was vaccine in town at all.

Cholera occurs sporadically throughout the Mediterranean, but as the protection you get from a jab lasts for only six months you must decide whether it is worthwhile. A combined tetanus–cholera innoculation can be done. The last bad epidemic occurred in 1973 in Italy, probably from mussels infected by raw sewage, but since then there have been few outbreaks and these have been rapidly contained. Hepatitis is another hazard, although cases are not that frequent in the Mediterranean, probably no more than in the UK. A gamma globulin injection gives you some protection over a six month period and is well worth considering in areas of poor hygiene, or where you might eat contaminated food.

Protection against malaria is a tricky matter. The countries around the Mediterranean have taken giant steps since World War II to wipe out malaria, but nonetheless the DHSS recommends you take precautions in Turkey, Syria, Lebanon, Egypt, Libya, Tunisia, Algeria and Morocco. Despite this advice, most travellers to these countries do not take drugs for the prevention of malaria and it is rarely contracted. The proprietary treatments (Proguanil, Paludrine, Chloroquine, Maloprim and Fansidar) can be taken on a daily or a weekly basis as directed, but with all of them it is important to continue the treatment for a month after you have left the area. Malaria is a debilitating, persistent disease, so take the matter seriously.

Before you go, stock up on any special drugs you are taking such as medication for angina, diabetes, steroid treatment and the like. If you are on the contraceptive pill, go and see your doctor who will ensure you have adequate supplies. Although most drugs are available, in fact more freely available as many of them can be bought directly over the counter without a prescription, they will often not be under the same brand name and in the case of the contraceptive pill may not be what you are used to. Again, you should consult your local GP on all of the preceding advice and follow his recommendations for your own particular medical problems and precautions. It could be useful to have official looking prescriptions for any 'serious' drugs carried, especially painkillers or stimulants, if only to show that they are for your own use.

If you wear spectacles or contact lenses, carry a spare pair or two. Sailing can be hard on glasses. You can't carry too many spare pairs of eyes, and if you are likely to be abroad for an extended stay take the optical prescription as well, so replacements can be made locally. Remember, too, that the loss of contact lenses or glasses is often excluded in travel insurance policies.

Finally, don't forget to take your favourite nostrum, charm or tablets for keeping seasickness at bay. Sturgeron is now widely accepted as one of the best of the anti-seasickness tablets: it does not produce as much drowsiness and lack of concentration as some of the other tablets, and appears to work effectively for more people. There are several other effective, faster acting and cheaper pills available, such as Kwells which may be more suitable than Sturgeron for short passages. With all anti-seasickness tablets, remember to take them at least the recommended amount of time in advance, usually two hours, to continue them at the prescribed intervals, and that you should avoid drinking alcohol at the same time. Women on contraceptive pills should take care to avoid an unexpected pregnancy if they are prone to seasickness: there is a good possibility that the sea and not your body will be the recipient of the pill. Find the seasickness pills that work best for you: there is a good deal of variation between different people in their reactions to and the effectiveness of different brands.

Some Common Health Hazards

Diarrhoea

The most common problem in the Mediterranean is travellers' diarrhoea, that unfortunate ailment known by a variety of colourful names: Gippy Tummy, Paella Belly, Turkish Quickstep, Montezuma's Revenge and other unprintable names. The causes are various and usually untraceable except in severe and widespread cases. Normally it will last only a day or two and can be attributed to a change in climate, a change in cuisine especially where oil is unsparingly used in the preparation of food, a surfeit of food or alcohol (usually the latter), or most commonly to the change in local bacteria in the food and water to which your body may take several days to adjust. Washing and peeling foods is a sensible precaution.

If you do succumb, the best treatment is to eat little or nothing and drink plenty of fluids – except for alcohol and milk. Simply giving your digestive system a rest from solid food is preferable to anti-diarrhoeal tablets and patent medicines that block you up solid. But if the diarrhoea persists, try Lomotil or codeine phosphate tablets. The main danger from a severe attack of diarrhoea is loss of body water and the attendant loss of important salts. Scientists at America's Centre for Disease Control recommend the following cocktail in such cases:

Glass No. 1: fruit juice, half a tablespoon of honey or syrup (for glucose), a pinch of table salt. Glass No. 2: boiled water, quarter of a tablespoon of baking soda. Sip alternately from the two glasses and take fizzy drinks, and tea.

Despite the tablets, if the diarrhoea continues for more than a few days, is accompanied by severe vomiting, or blood is evacuated with the faeces, then you should consult a doctor. Diabetics should take extra care to avoid the condition in the first place, as it upsets their sugar balance.

Water

Drinking water is often blamed for a variety of ills ranging from diarrhoea to cholera and typhoid. Samuel Butler reckoned that 'When the water of a place is bad, it is safest to drink none that has not been filtered through either the berry of a grape, or else a tub of malt.' In most of the countries around the Mediterranean the water is safe to drink from officially designated potable sources, although initially your digestive system may have to cope with strange local bacteria in the water, possibly resulting in that diarrhoea again. If you have a delicate tummy or you are on a short visit, use boiled or bottled water. Babies and young children should drink only bottled or sterilised fluids on a short stay in the Mediterranean as their digestive systems may not adapt to local bacteria during this time, and the consequences can be serious in their cases. It is interesting that advancing age renders you less susceptible to the local bacteria.

If you are on an extended visit to the Mediterranean, I don't recommend regularly drinking bottled water, an affectation practised by local people eating out but not usually continued at home. On any extended visit you will encounter the local water in the form of ice, it is used in cooking and to wash vegetables and fruit, so unless you eschew all these there is not much point to drinking bottled water. And worse, the plastic bottles add to the garbage that must be disposed of – sadly, some into the sea.

Water from cisterns and wells must always be treated as unsafe for drinking. Water which is considered suspect for some reason can be purified by boiling. Water boiled

Water. Is it safe? If in doubt treat

vigorously for at least ten minutes will kill most organisms. Chemical treatment is not as effective as boiling but will kill most nasties. Puritabs or Halazone tablets used as directed will get rid of the more common organisms, but not those which cause dysentery and some enteroviruses. The water tanks in a boat can be purified by bleach solution (5% hypochlorite to a gallon of water). Water purification tablets and adding bleach to water leaves a chlorinated aftertaste which doesn't do anything for the taste of tea or coffee, however.

If you are in an area where the water is not safe, remember that the ice in your drink or icebox, the water that washed the vegetables for the salad, the water the fruit was washed in and the water you brush your teeth with, will all be the same unsafe water. After reading all this it is easy to scare yourself over the purity of the water in the Mediterranean, but let me assure you that I and many others have been drinking it for years with impunity.

good awning is essential to keep the sun off you for some of the time.

Sunburn

One of the things you are going to the Mediterranean for is the sun. Clear blue skies and a warm climate. However, it is one of the things you must beware of, especially when you first arrive. It can burn, scar and make you ill unless you take precautions; often you will not notice the full effect of the sun because a breeze, real or apparent, will disguise it. Ultraviolet rays, the ones that do the burning, filter through cloud cover, so you can get burnt even when you think you won't.

A little forethought on equipping yourself for the sun will help you enjoy rather than resent it. Use sun-tan cream in preference to oil: decks get slippery, woodwork and cushion covers get stained, and you fry with oil. Sun-tan creams are graded by a screen factor from 2 to 15: the higher the number the more protection you get, with a factor 15 cream totally blocking the sun's effect. If you have a fair skin start on a high number and work down as you build up a tan. An ultraviolet barrier cream such as Sun-bloc or Uvistat will stop any ultraviolet getting through and is particularly useful for extremities: the nose, lips, forehead, feet, cheekbones and any other parts of the body that get too much sun too quickly. Use a 'chap-stick' to stop the sun and wind drying and cracking the lips. When you first arrive in the Mediterranean, build up a tan gradually and in between times keep in the shade and wear light cotton trousers and a long-sleeved shirt. Pyjamas are useful if you have nothing else, and in parts of Turkey and North Africa you will look like one of the locals. A hat or sun-visor and sunglasses completes the ensemble. I find the sunglasses with dark Polaroid lenses designed for the chic on the ski-slopes provide the best protection for sun-sensitive eyes. Reactolite or other photo-chromatic glasses are recommended by some opticians so that your eyes do not get 'lazy' behind dark glasses all day.

When swimming, beware of the sun when floating idly around or snorkelling. It is not a bad idea to wear a T-shirt, particularly children, when snorkelling since it is all too easy to forget about the effect of the sun with water lapping over you and cooling the skin. After you have been swimming, drying salt water leaves little crystals of salt on your body which act as miniature lenses to concentrate the sun onto little patches of skin to irritate and possibly damage it. The remedy is simply to rinse off with a little fresh water, and then dry off in the sun.

If you do get burned, calamine lotion or cream soothes the skin; but if you get badly burnt to a bright lobster red you may need to see a doctor for further advice. Whatever you do, don't expose yourself to the sun until you are completely recovered.

Heat Exhaustion and Dehydration
Heat exhaustion and sun-stroke sometimes afflict those rash souls not used to a lot of sun, who insist on getting as much of it as soon as they can. Heat exhaustion can occur by the body simply being too hot or through dehydration. In the hot sun you lose a great deal of moisture through sweating, but may not notice it in the cooling winds. First symptoms are often a headache followed by listlessness, dizziness and nausea. The patient should be kept cool with cold water and ice-packs, given plenty of fluids especially fruit juices, and given an aspirin to lower his temperature and relieve the headache that frequently accompanies heat exhaustion.

From the era of the great white hunter on safari we have inherited the idea of salt loss being an important factor in heat exhaustion. Salt tablets are rarely needed as you normally take in more than enough salt in your everyday diet to replace that lost when you sweat. In hot climates your body acclimatises to produce almost salt-free perspiration, so salt loss is minimised.

Children and Babies
Children and babies enjoy sailing in the Mediterranean and cope well with the travel and change in routine, but you must always remember to think for them. They are more prone to sunburn and dehydration than adults, but will not necessarily be able to say for themselves if they suffer from either. As some babies' skins can burn even in the shade, it is wise to keep them lightly covered most of the time. Small children should wear T shirts when swimming until well tanned. As for adults, tanning should be gradual: start off with say an hour uncovered the first day, then gradually increase the exposure. Continually apply a high UV-screening factor sun-cream, particularly after swimming, and also have available a continuous supply of bottled drinks such as water, lemonade or Coke. Snappishness or irritability in a small child often simply means it needs a drink or is too hot: buckets of water poured over them in the cockpit can work wonders.

...hen swimming or snorkeling it is all too easy to forget about the effect of the sun with cool water ...ping over you. Children should wear a T-shirt.

To cope with the altered routine of staying up later at night, a small child may need extra sleep during the day. A boat under way often lulls the child sufficiently to sleep for an hour or so, giving the parents a well-earned break.

In order to avoid tummy upsets, children and babies should drink only bottled and sterilised fluids, and eat only peeled fruit and vegetables. On a short visit the lack of salads will not harm a child, but on a longer visit make up a special salad of peeled vegetables and then gradually introduce the local cuisine.

Unwelcome Visitors

Not the two-legged variety but the six-legged and winged creatures. In the Mediterranean climate flies, mosquitoes, gnats, wasps and cockroaches thrive, and at certain times of the year can be a nuisance on a boat.

Flies are a nuisance and little else. Keep food covered and the galley clean, and hatches and ports open. Flies don't like a breeze blowing through the boat and will eventually leave if it is well ventilated. At sea close the hatches and spray with a pesticide down below, then open them up again after five minutes or so. The flies that aren't dead will leave smartly.

The whine and nip of a mosquito can be intensely annoying at night. A few individuals suffer badly from the bites and they should take extra care. The most practical solution is to fit screens to keep the mosquitoes out; wire frames with fine mesh on them can be constructed slightly oversize for hatches and ports so that when fitted they are held in place by the tension of the wire springing outwards. With a screen you get ventilation without mosquitoes.

Insect repellants are the easiest solution and work well for several hours, enabling you to get to sleep even if you are bitten afterwards. Oil of citronella works as well as proprietary brands such as Autan, as long as you can stand the peculiar smell – I'm hooked on it now. The mosquito coils which are lit and then smoulder away to produce an insect-repelling fog quickly create a fug inside small boats, but are useful if you are sitting in the cockpit of an evening. Inside, choose between suffocation or the mosquitoes.

If you are bitten, calamine lotion works as well as anything to reduce the swelling and irritation. In some cases an antihistamine cream can be used, but you should consult with your GP before leaving as antihistamines can create longer-term difficulties in some individuals. Refrain from scratching itchy bites or you may cause an infection in what is an otherwise innocuous nip.

Gnats can also be irritating at night; deal with them in the same way as outlined for mosquitoes. Apparently mosquitoes and gnats only fly against the wind to a boat anchored out, although whether this is because they can 'smell' warm-blooded mammals when the wind is blowing onshore or whether it has something to do with their navigation I don't know.

In some areas wasps can be bothersome in the daytime, though they disappear at night. They are particularly unwelcome because of their aggressive behaviour and the fact that you can't just swat them like a fly or mosquito. Attempting to swat a wasp only infuriates it, and the only way to cope is to ignore them and remove all food and drink, especially fruit, jams, meats and sugary drinks. If you are stung, dab the wound with vinegar or calamine lotion; or use Wasp-eze, an aerosol spray available from the large chemists and also useful for mosquito bites, nettle stings, bee and jellyfish stings. However, as it contains antihistamines check with your doctor before using it.

Scuttling, furtive cockroaches are unwelcome simply because of their noisy presence and the possibility that they spread disease, although the latter danger may have been exaggerated in the past. Getting rid of cockroaches is a good deal more difficult than preventing them getting aboard in the first place. Always berth stern-to or bows-to when possible, not alongside, and keep the gangplank slightly raised off the quay so cockroaches cannot stroll on board. Cardboard boxes may have eggs laid between the folds, and young cockroaches feed on the glue, so do not bring them on board. Once a female or eggs are on board the population increases rapidly. Unload your provisions on the quay and bring them aboard without their packaging.

The only sure way to get rid of roaches is to have the whole boat fumigated, and since the toxic fumes are bad for human beings as well, everyone will have to be off the boat for a day. Other remedies enjoy varying success rates. In some Mediterranean countries you can buy 'Roach Hotels', a small fold-up box with a bait they can't resist and a sticky floor they can't move from once they go for the bait. You can also get a bait that cockroaches like which contains boric acid: the acid is said to crystallize in the digestive system and pierce the gut of the unfortunate creature. Insect sprays only tend to slow them up, which is useful for crushing the little beggars but won't get at a quickly multiplying brood tucked away somewhere in the bowels of the boat.

In the end, the best remedy is prevention.

Rabies Unfortunately this disease is prevalent in some of the countries around the Mediterranean, although you are unlikely to encounter it. Any dog displaying abnormal behaviour, especially unnatural tameness, should be avoided. Not only dogs, but cats, foxes, squirrels, bats, monkeys and rodents can carry the disease, so animal lovers should curtail their normal affections for every stray animal that wants to make friends with them. If bitten, immediate treatment consists of flushing out the wound with soap and water, or even water alone, followed by applying iodine solution. The victim should then seek medical advice as soon as possible. If rabies is suspected you may need to undergo the six-dose course of treatment with the Merieux vaccine. The old painful multi-injection treatment is now rare, but might still be offered in the less developed countries.

If you are making an extended stay in places where rabies is a real risk, you can take a pre-exposure course of three injections followed by boosters every three years.

7
Marine Life

When you first slip into the warm waters of the Mediterranean with a mask and snorkel, you will probably be disappointed: there is not the profusion of marine life you expected. Trailing a spinner behind the boat catches nothing for days. Is something wrong with the lure, or are there no fish? In the restaurants, you will be agog at the price of fish compared to anything else. You must surely mutter that you had thought this was a sea teeming with marine life, home of the *bouillabaisse*; where the ancient Greeks gambolled with dolphins and Roman writers expounded on the delights of the seafood in Mare Nostrum, the sea where Aristotle virtually invented marine biology and 2000 years later Jacques Cousteau popularised it. Where is it all?

The Mediterranean has never been rich in marine life. It is a sea that has been written about, studied, fished and sailed on for thousands of years. Its marine life has long been described and illustrated, and the peoples around the shores have been experimenting with fish recipes literally since Moses came down from the mountain, and probably longer. The Romans exalted in seafood and their descendants continue to produce fish dishes both novel and tasty. But that doesn't mean there is or ever has been much fish around, rather that it has always been prized. In the Pacific, Atlantic and Indian Oceans there is an abundance of fish, and the coral reefs of the Red Sea make the Mediterranean look like a desert, which in a way it is.

The much-vaunted blueness and clarity of the Mediterranean results from it being poor in plankton, the basis of the marine ecosystem. Plankton is scarcest in the eastern basin; the western basin is boosted by the inflow of less saline water and Atlantic plankton through the Straits of Gibraltar. Man as usual has managed to complicate the picture with the construction of the Aswan Dam in 1964. Formerly the Nile brought valuable nutrients into the eastern basin, and 20,000 tons of sardines were caught annually by Egyptian boats. Now the dam holds back the river water to fertilise the land and the catch has dropped to 1000 tons annually. The Egyptians get more crops but fewer sardines.

A second important reason for the paucity of marine life is the relatively small area of continental shelf. Below 200 metres there is not the wealth of marine life that lives in shallower waters, and in most of the Mediterranean the depths drop away quickly to more than this. Two exceptions are the northern half of the Adriatic and a shelf off the eastern coast of Tunisia, which are comparatively prolific. Below 300 metres the water in the Mediterranean is not as cold as the icy temperatures found in the Atlantic and Pacific but is a relatively warm 13° C. This might seem to favour marine life in the depths of the

re nautilus, the delicate sea snail.

sea, but in fact it does not. The water at these depths is very salty as well as warm, and such water cannot hold very much dissolved oxygen: the result again means a scarcity of fish life compared to the oceans.

The Mediterranean's weak fish population has also been harvested for thousands of years. Until recently some of the fishing practices were not exactly helping conservation. In Greece and Turkey you may notice that a few of the older fishermen are minus a hand or an arm: it was probably lost dynamiting for fish, when the fuse was underestimated by a second or two and the dynamite exploded just before it was dropped into the sea. After the Second World War there were a lot of explosives around and it seemed an easier way to fish than setting nets or long-lines. Unfortunately a dynamite blast under the water kills everything in the immediate vicinity – in effect it totally destroys a small part of an ecosystem – though only some of the fish killed by the blast float up to the surface while the rest decompose on the bottom. Today, the biggest problem is not dynamite but small-mesh nets and amateurs spearfishing. Where the fisherman leaves off, the holiday diver with mask, snorkel and speargun has sufficient time on his hands to go after almost anything that moves, and frequently he does, bringing in undersized fish and lobster.

After this, you must now be wondering if there is anything at all in the way of marine life. There is, and on a boat you are close to it all and if you know where to look there is a good deal to see in the water. Ashore in the fish markets there are species not normally encountered outside the Mediterranean. If you get the chance, try some of the unusual fish dishes in the restaurants: Italian cooks have a flair for combining seafood with other ingredients to produce some of the best dishes in the Mediterranean. Before you go, arm yourself with a guide to the marine life such as the *Hamlyn Guide to the Flora and Fauna of the Mediterranean Sea* or Tegwyn Harris' *The Natural History of the Mediterranean*. If you are a seafood gourmet add Alan Davidson's *Mediterranean Seafood*. Although the following section looks at what exists where, there is simply not enough space here to classify and describe all the marine life you might come across.

Sand, Rocks, Mud and the Sea

Sandy Shores

Holiday companies know how strong the allure of sandy beaches is, and brochures for the Mediterranean often show long, deserted sandy shores stretching into the distance. In fact there are not that many sandy beaches in the Mediterranean and holiday-makers looking for them would be better advised to head for the shores of the Atlantic or Indian Oceans. Sandy beaches need large waves rolling in and depositing the stuff on the shore. In the Mediterranean this mainly occurs along the North African coast, although small coves facing the prevailing wind may acquire a small sandy strip.

The sandy shore is a difficult habitat and there is really very little marine life to be found on it. The absence of any real tide in the Mediterranean exacerbates the problem. In tidal waters the diurnal ebb and flow brings in food for shore-dwellers, but here this doesn't occur. There is no prolific intertidal zone.

A number of molluscs do inhabit sandy shores. Some are vegetarian filter feeders sifting the water for microscopic food particles, while others are carnivores burrowing into the sand, often to attack their filter-feeding cousins. Of the latter, the most famous is the dye murex, *Bolinus brandaris*, the little spiral mollusc that Phoenicians, Greeks and Romans gathered in large quantities to prepare the royal purple dye denoting high rank. Such was the scale of the industry that at one time it was said that the beaches of the Levant and Greece were covered with piles of old murex shells.

a fished for thousands of years.

Most sand dwellers are burrowers that escape from predators by living under the sand, or in turn hide there just buried to wait for food to come along. Many of the sand burrowers, the polychaete worms and molluscs, will not be seen unless you dig them up. In the case of the lesser and greater weevers, two related fish that burrow into the sand, this can be dangerous as they have venomous spines which they raise to protect themselves when threatened. Should you accidentally tread on one, the dorsal spine can inject poison which can cause a painful injury.

On many sandy shores the marine grasses, the same plants that can make it difficult to get an anchor into the bottom, create a jungle habitat for various animals. Numerous species of small fish, the small breams, saupe, blennies and the bogue (with the amusing generic name *Boops boops*), are common, and a patient fisherman can try to catch a breed of fish who appear to have absorbed the wisdom of Solomon when it comes to getting bait off hooks without getting caught. On some grassy bottoms the harmless and fascinating seahorse will be seen, an evolutionary dead-end that is probably endangered most by the new inhabitants of the sandy shore swimming around with mask and snorkel. More commonly the seahorse's cousin, the pipefish, will be seen snaking across the surface at dusk.

Rocky Shores

It is around the rocky shores that the wealth of marine life in the Mediterranean is to be found. For the most part the coast is a rocky one where cliffs drop sheer into the sea and rocky promontories crumble gradually into it. Often the capes and headlands provide a spectacular cross-section of the tremendous metamorphic forces that buckled and compressed the land. Different types of rock – granite, sandstones, schist, basalt – are folded together at different angles within a short distance of one another. At sea level waves have pounded and eroded the rock, forming clefts and caves and pillars of the harder rock, shapes fantastic and caves often spectacular such as the miles of caverns and grottoes at Diros in Greece. But below sea level, below the pounding of the waves, there is a stable habitat for marine life. The relatively small tidal range ensures the constant conditions of the sub-littoral world and here a wide variety of marine life flourishes.

The large brown seaweeds, the green species and the delicate red ones grow prolifically. Various sponges, sea anemones, worms and fixed filter feeders shelter in them, and crustaceans and small fish in turn live among the sponges and seaweeds. A number of weird and wonderful invertebrates inhabit this world. One of the common beasties is the sea hare, a greeny-brown flabby creature who moves around by slowly flapping its 'wings' like a miniature manta ray. When disturbed it emits a deep purple dye into the water. Other related species belonging to the sea hares and sea slugs have exotic purple bodies with yellow spots, or white bodies with orange spots and long feathery tentacles, or red and yellow bodies and what appears to be a sea anemone on the back: this genus provide some of the weirdest and most colourful sights to be seen around a rocky coast.

At dusk the rocky shores get positively overpopulated as all manner of animals move into shallower waters looking for food. The octopus is commonly found near the surface and is easily caught. Like the monkey in the Asiatic monkey trap, which will not unclench its fist to let food go even when in danger of being caught, the octopus will not let go of what might be food on the end of a line until too late – usually when it has been hauled up and into the boat. Larger fish such as the grouper, morays, the larger breams, and rays also move into shallower waters at dusk. Small fishing boats, the *lampera* or *peche-a-la-lumiere* with bright gas lamps, potter around the shallow waters from dusk until midnight capitalising on this influx of fish.

...largest fish in the photograph is a weever whose dorsal spines can inject a powerful poison. ...etheless it is considered an essential ingredient of bouillabaisse.

One common but not very welcome inhabitant of the rocky shore is the sea urchin, the most common being the black sea urchin, *Arbacia lixula*. On some rocky shores there are literally thousands of the little beasts, and it is prudent and much less painful to wear an old pair of plimsoles if wandering or swimming around an infested area. The sea urchins can nibble their way into soft rock and will even collect pebbles on the outside to disguise themselves from predators. Another common inhabitant is the common limpet. The Italians eat them straight off the rocks: a sharp knife extracts them from the shell, a squeeze of lemon and straight down. A bottle of cold white wine assuages the salt and citric flavoured white flesh.

The much sought after crayfish, netted and potted so persistently for the table that there are not m̶
around anymore.

Rather less common than the humble limpet are lobsters and crayfish. Over the years these crustaceans have been netted and potted so persistently for restaurant tables that there are not many of them around anymore. One of the more unusual crustaceans you may be presented with in a restaurant, particularly in Turkey, is the flapjack lobster, a bizarre flattened and horny version of a lobster known as the *cigale* in France, but not to be turned down – it is every bit as good as lobster proper.

Estuaries

All of the estuaries in the Mediterranean are river deltas. The virtual absence of tides to carry silt away means that it is deposited at the river mouths to form deltas that continue to grow. The Camargue, the huge swampy wilderness around the Rhone, is just such a delta; similarly, the shores of the northern Adriatic around the Po. Nearby in the Black Sea the spectacular Danube delta covers over 4500 square kilometres and is estimated to grow 24 metres to seaward annually.

The major river deltas are difficult for human beings to develop and consequently abound with wildlife. They are frequently the winter home for birds or a stopover for migrants on their way to or from North Africa. Marine life is found not so much in the swampy areas but in the region between the fresh water and the sea. The rich sediment brought down is food for numbers of marine dwellers not in abundance elsewhere. Scallops and cockles are commonly found, as well as the large, orange fan mussel; there are flatfish such as plaice, flounder and sole, and rays such as monkfish, thornback, stingray and skate. Less commonly the sturgeon, the wonderfully armoured fish that produces the little black eggs some of us pay large amounts of money for, is found in the brackish water of the estuaries in the eastern Mediterranean and the Black Sea. Your chances of catching one are slim, though, as fishing rights are strictly controlled and rigidly enforced.

The Open Sea

While sailing across the sea in a yacht you are closer to the water and more aware of things in and on it than when on a ship. From large ships the sea usually appears deserted; on a yacht you know this is not so.

Sea birds, particularly the shearwater and gulls, are a good clue to something going on. Dolphins and tuna create a great deal of mess when they are rounding up fish and feeding, leaving fish bits or even small fish for the sea birds to scavenge. If you see a number of sea birds wheeling and diving over the sea there is every chance that dolphins or tuna are feeding, unless some ship has recently passed and dumped a load of edible garbage into the sea.

Another commonly encountered large fish is the swordfish. In the early summer tuna and swordfish migrate into the Mediterranean to spawn, many going all the way up to the Black Sea. For some reason swordfish like to rest on the surface and a yacht under sail will surprise them. There is an explosion of water as this magnificent fish leaps into the air and a resounding smack as it falls back. This habit of basking on the surface is used to good advantage by commercial fishermen, particularly in Italy and Spain, who creep up on the creature enjoying its innocent pleasures and harpoon it. Boats with bowsprits twice the length of the boat and a mast just as high have evolved for just this purpose. The skipper at the top of the mast guides the boat towards the swordfish and the harpooner at the end of the bowsprit does his job before the swordfish even realises a boat is around.

Sharks always pop up in any conversation about the sea, and the simple answer for the Mediterranean is that nearly all the common species are found there including the great white, the hammerhead and the blue shark. Having said that, it is highly unlikely you will see one except if a fisherman brings it in. After ten years in the Mediterranean I have positively identified a shark in the water on only three occasions. Commonly dolphin or tuna are mistaken for shark. Even the tail of the innocuous sunfish (also called headfish) has been mistaken for the dorsal fin of a shark: not until closer inspection is the owner of the 'fin' identified as a sunfish, probably the least deadly denizen of the deep.

What you will see are jellyfish of one variety or another. Most of these are species such as the dirty brown *Pelagia* or the cauliflower-like *Cotylorhiza tubercalata*. Occasionally you will see the beautiful silver-blue and red sail and purple body of the Portuguese man-o-war, with powerful stinging cells trailing up to 30 metres under it. Superficially similar is the By-The-Wind-Sailor, a smaller distant cousin except for the important difference that it does not have long trailing tentacles. Both species do not actually drift passively downwind with their sails, but angle them to progress on something approaching a broad

reach. Apart from covering more ground (even in a light breeze a Portuguese man-o-war can cover 10 kilometres in a day), it is thought that the evolutionary value of this ability is to avoid all the other organisms and marine flotsam that drift downwind, something especially important for the Portuguese man-o-war which could otherwise get its tentacles tangled in floating debris.

One might think that jellyfish were more or less immune to predators, but in fact several animals prey on them. The sunfish quite happily gobbles them up sting and all. More unusual is the Nautilus, a delicate purple sea snail whose striking purple shell you may find washed up on the shore. It floats on a raft of slimy mucous bubbles and on coming into contact with a jellyfish immediately starts feeding on it. Another unlikely predator is the leathery turtle, which cruises around snapping up jellyfish and salps. The more common loggerhead turtle sticks to crustaceans and molluscs although it has a predilection now and then for grazing on sea urchins.

Pollution

It has frequently been stated that pollution in the Mediterranean has reached such levels that the sea can be described as dead or dying. It is neither, but it does face a particular set of problems from the pollutants that get into its waters, and in common with the other oceans and seas of the world there is no room for complacency. It is an enclosed sea that takes around 180 years to renew its waters. The bottom current flowing out into the Atlantic over the sill at Gibraltar takes a negligible amount of the pollutants out of the sea, consequently most of what is dumped or runs into it remains there.

The most visible pollution is from hydrocarbons: tar, crude oil, diesel and light petroleum products. Tankers flushing out their tanks at sea, spillage at loading and refining installations, and dumping and the pumping of oily bilges discharge an estimated half a million tons of oil into the Mediterranean annually. Despite the introduction of laws prohibiting tankers from washing tanks at sea and the heavy fines for offending ships caught doing so, this remains the biggest source of hydrocarbon pollution and the one that must be eliminated as soon as possible. Hydrocarbon pollution has a particularly nasty although non-toxic effect on sand beaches where the prevailing wind dumps tar, such as along the Algerian coast and the Adriatic corridor. Other bad spots are around oil loading or off-loading installations such as around Marseilles, Genoa, Fiumicino, Trieste, Piraeus, Thessaloniki, Istanbul, Mersin, Tripoli, Algiers and many more too numerous to list.

While tar is a visible pollutant, and there are few beaches in the world not blighted by tar to some extent, there are other invisible pollutants which can be more dangerous. The major European rivers draining into the Mediterranean bring toxic industrial effluents to the sea: heavy metals, pesticides and insecticides, detergents and other dangerous chemicals as well as fertilizers from land drainage. At the bottom of an ecosystem, where filter feeders such as molluscs accumulate heavy metals or insecticides, the level may be acceptable, but an animal eating say ten molluscs a day will accumulate ten times as much of the pollutant, and so on up the chain to the large fishes which build up unacceptable amounts. These can in turn be ingested by humans, who may find them more toxic than the fish did. A major chemical accident can drastically affect an ecosystem for years after the chemical has been cleaned up and the levels in the water reduced to acceptable amounts: it remains in the marine organisms themselves. In many ways chemical pollution is the most dangerous although the least visible, and much needs to be done to tighten up on the dumping of effluent in rivers often hundreds of miles from the sea.

ancient Greeks believed dolphins
e men who had taken to the water
; ago and consequently did not doubt
r intelligence nor wonder at their
ndliness.

As well as hydrocarbon and chemical pollution there is the problem of sewage. The shores of the Mediterranean have always been highly populated and levels of sewage discharged into the sea have risen with the numbers of tourists. As one newspaperman acidly commented, 'You don't swim off the Costa Brava, you merely go through the motions.' Much of the sewage enters the sea untreated and while it may be considered a 'natural' pollutant, at high levels it upsets an ecosystem. What happens is that the sewage acts as a fertiliser, stimulating high growth in plants and animals at the bottom end of the ecosystem. Oxygen gets used up at such a rate that eventually nothing can survive and the whole ecosystem collapses, killing most of the organisms. Too much in the way of nutrients is as bad as too little.

After this picture of doom and destruction I must put the problem of pollution in the Mediterranean in perspective. Overall the sea has stood up to pollution better than other enclosed seas such as the Baltic. One of the reasons for this, is that it is what the experts call an oligotrophic sea, an impoverished sea. Its low plankton levels and relative paucity of marine life at all levels has meant that it can recover more quickly from the effects of pollutants than other seas with initially richer marine life. Even compared to the Atlantic it has fared only slightly less well in some respects. A recent survey of British beaches showed that the sewage levels of some of the popular beaches such as Blackpool were just as bad as the worst levels in the Mediterranean. None of this means we can be complacent about the Mediterranean, as no sea can cope with increasing pollution indefinitely.

Until recently little was being done. In 1975 UNESCO finally managed to get 17 of the 18 countries around the Mediterranean together to form a joint plan to attack the problem. The convention signed by the countries provided for legislation against the dumping of pollutants, scientific research and monitoring programmes, economic and social planning requirements, and guidance for future expansion. The signatory states all provide finance for this plan and the EEC also contributes. Millions of pounds have already gone into sewage treatment plants, into monitoring the dumping of industrial wastes and fining offending companies, and into providing onshore flushing facilities for oil tankers. It is a start, but much remains to be done and the governing body of the convention needs legislative teeth to really attack the problem and those who offend the laws already in force. It is difficult to break the habits of centuries where relatively small populations dumped waste into the sea. A glaring example of this is in Greece and Turkey where the ferries and fishing boats have traditionally dumped their garbage into the sea. When the numbers of boats doing this were small and the gash was largely composed of bio-degradable material, the impact was relatively light. Now that there are more boats and the gash has a large component of non-bio-degradable material, mostly plastic, the impact on the sea is much greater: although it is illegal to dump into the sea in both of these countries, the old habits rule and the law is blatantly disregarded.

Regulations concerning yachts have been few and far between. Holding tanks are required on charter boats, and it is illegal to pump out a toilet or release detergent into a harbour. In France the use of anti-fouling paints containing organic tin compounds is banned because of the adverse effects of such chemicals on shellfish. No thinking yachtsman should dump garbage of any sort into a harbour, and at sea only bio-degradable material should be thrown over the side. Oily bilges should be swabbed out and waste oil dumped ashore. Most marinas and harbours have rubbish bins and often will have special containers for waste oil and the like. Use them.

This is not to discourage you from going to the Mediterranean: after all, pollution is an unpleasant fact of life wherever we sail. It remains an idyllic sea, one that no photograph can reproduce; a magic sea that those of us who travel on it should take care not to stain.

Dangerous Marine Animals

It is possible to give the impression that the sea is literally full of nasty creatures just waiting for the opportunity to inflict injury. Nothing could be less true. Caution is necessary because the sea does contain dangerous animals, and is itself dangerous to our mammalian lungs which are not happy when filled with seawater. But compared to the land with its bacterial and viral diseases, insects, rats, poisonous animals and plants, it is far less dangerous. And these natural dangers are nothing compared to the man-made dangers we continually expose ourselves to.

Sharks These sleek, efficient machines are the greatest fear of swimmers, yet the chances of seeing one let alone being attacked are rare. Films like *Jaws* and its imitators have produced a phobia that is out of all proportion to the threat. Roger Caras succinctly sums up the danger in his *Dangerous to Man*: 'They kill nowhere near the number of people that snakes do, only a fraction as many as are killed by lightning, and fewer in ten years, worldwide, than die in motor accidents in the United States on a single Fourth of July or Labor Day weekend.'

Sharks do not habitually attack man, indeed they tend to shy away from such encounters. They are indeed dangerous and not to be underestimated or trusted, but they do not seek out man to attack him in the water. Most instances have been in murky water where the visibility was bad, and appear to be cases where the shark thought a man was some other kind of food. If you see a shark, it is of course silly to stay in the water: get out as quickly as possible but without panic. If you are spearfishing do not trail bleeding fish on a line and if a shark approaches let him have the fish while you depart quietly. A shark can smell blood from a quarter of a mile away and home in on it with unerring accuracy – to the shark, blood means food.

There are many suggestions on how to scare off a shark although no evidence that any of them work. A shark intent on getting to something is a primitive machine that is difficult and sometimes impossible to dissuade from its purpose. You can try shouting underwater, charging at the shark to call its bluff or releasing a sudden stream of bubbles. Always face it and if it comes too close hit it with an object, but not your hand. A shark's placoid scales are as sharp as its teeth and hitting or rubbing against it is likely to draw blood (yours), which is the last thing you want. Always your intention should be to exit from its environment into your own as quickly and quietly as possible.

Moray eels Two species inhabit the Mediterranean, *Muraena helena* being the most common; it has a brown body dappled with yellow and can grow to $1\frac{1}{2}$ metres in length. The moray is not aggressive and the danger comes from accidentally intruding on its home. It inhabits crevices in rocks, wrecks and amphorae, anchoring most of its body inside with the head and about a third of its length poking out looking for food. Should you not see the eel, or unintentionally molest it, it will bite you. It has a formidable array of teeth but the jaws are not large so the bite rarely does much damage. Any bite should be treated to stop secondary infection, which is likely to be more dangerous than the bite itself.

Swordfish Although there are reports of dinghies being run through and sunk by infuriated swordfish, there are no authenticated cases in the Mediterranean. In my experience of working on Italian swordfishing boats and seeing these creatures from a yacht, they appear to shy away from man and have a great deal more to fear from us than we do from them.

their way to and from their breeding
unds in the Black Sea, swordfish are
ght in the Mediterranean. Because the
ordfish follow set migration routes
ge numbers can be easily caught at
tain times of the year.

Octopus In hoary old tales of the sea the octopus is the eight-armed monster which upsets small boats and holds divers under the water until they drown. I can still see the malevolent beast, with beady evil eyes on a prospective dinner in the form of a pearl diver, in an illustration from a *Boy's Own Annual.* While there may have been accidental deaths of this kind, there are no authenticated records of an octopus drowning anyone. The only possible danger is if it should nip you with its small parrot-like beak. Some species inject a mild venom, which in the Mediterranean species is like a bad jellyfish sting. Normally the octopus is a shy, retiring animal intent on keeping out of the way of dangerous humans.

from being a dangerous denizen of the deep, octopus are shy, retiring animals with much to fear
n man.

In the Mediterranean there are four species; the Common octopus, *Octopus vulgaris*, is the one most often seen. These interesting cephalopods are caught in thousands every year, for octopus grilled, deep-fried, charcoal grilled, with a vinaigrette, in soup, pickled with spices, in a casserole with cheese and tomatoes, and in many other different ways, is regarded quite rightly as good food. In some countries, Greece and Turkey in particular, there are restaurants serving nothing but octopus in a variety of tasty ways.

Stingrays It is estimated that the stingray causes more injuries to man than all of the other species of fish combined, though the injuries are all accidental in that the stingray is not aggressive but is reacting to being disturbed. The European variety *Dasyatis pastinaca* is common in the Mediterranean, usually inhabiting shallow water where the majority of injuries inevitably occur. If the fish is disturbed it lashes upwards with its tail where there is a barbed spine and the venom apparatus. The venom produces a throbbing, sharp or shooting pain in the area of the wound and may cause nausea, vomiting, rapid heartbeat, but rarely death. The victim should seek immediate medical help and in the meantime soak the wound, invariably on the foot or the leg, in very hot water. Hot water is believed to break down the proteins in the venom and since there are no known antidotes to most of these neurotoxins, that is the best you can do. Take care to avoid secondary infections and get a tetanus booster because tetanus bacillus is sometimes injected into the wound along with venom. When walking in shallow water where stingrays are known to be, wear shoes, shuffle your feet along the bottom and take a stick to poke ahead of you.

Weeverfish Two of the members of the family *Trachinidae* are commonly found in the Mediterranean. They are comparatively small fish which are caught for food in many countries. Indeed the weever is known to the French as the *vive* or *grand vive* and is considered essential for a good *bouillabaisse.* The danger from these fish comes from the venom they can inject through their dorsal and opercular spines. Like the stingray they lie half covered on the bottom and it is possible to accidentally step on one. Weevers can be aggressive in their territory but cannot come up and stab you with a spine. Care must be taken when they are netted in case you accidentally touch the spines.

The venom injected causes excruciating agony, although the story of a fisherman amputating his own finger to gain relief after being stabbed is probably apocryphal. The pain rapidly spreads to other parts of the body, commonly with nausea and vomiting. Rapid heartbeat and difficulty with breathing may also occur, but although several deaths have been reported none are authenticated. Bathe the wound in hot water and seek medical help as soon as possible.

Jellyfish Of all the animals described, those you are most likely to encounter are jellyfish. In certain years there can be a veritable plague of them and at such times, about every three or four years by my reckoning, it pays to choose your swimming spots carefully. The danger from jellyfish is from their stinging cells, which can cause anything from a mild itching sensation to the injection of a potent neurotoxin which in the case of the sea wasp can kill. Fortunately the sea wasp is rare in the Mediterranean.

All jellyfish sting, to immobilise their prey and protect themselves from predators, but the potency and amount of venom injected varies between species. They do not attack, but rather, as Roger Caras points out, sting anything they come into contact with: 'they pulse and float along ... waiting patiently to bump into something they can eat. They sting anything they encounter ... to avoid the sting, man has only to avoid the bump. While he may be able to depend on the fear, quiet good nature, or the escape 'reflexes' of other potentially dangerous animals, he cannot do this with jellyfish. He must learn to keep out of the way.'

The marine animal you are most likely to bump into. Even when stranded like this one they can still sting, so take care.

Aurelia aurita, the common jellyfish, has a saucer-shaped transparent body up to 10 cm across with four distinctive purple-violet crescents grouped around the centre. Four frilly mouth arms hang down from the body. It is not a vicious stinger; a light contact is like a nettle although prolonged contact can be more painful.

The compass jellyfish, *Chrysaora hysoscella*, also has a saucer-shaped transparent body with 16 characteristic radiating bands on top. Slender tentacles trail from the periphery and four mouth arms longer than the tentacles hang down from the centre. It is up to 30 cm across. As a stinger it is similar to the common jellyfish.

Pelagia noctiluca is a mushroom shaped jellyfish up to 10 cm across, and is light yellow-brown with 'warts' on top. Long trailing tentacles can inflict severe and painful stings.

Charybdea marsupialis or Mediterranean sea-wasp has a box-shaped transparent body up to 6 cm long with four tentacles up to 30 cm long. Can inflict severe and in some cases fatal stings. Luckily it is rarely encountered.

Rhizostoma pulmo has a dome-shaped body coloured blue-white-yellow and up to 90 cm across. Under the body are numerous mouth-arms fused into branches. Not known as a vicious stinger.

Cotylorhiza tubercalata is saucer shaped with an easily identified central dome up to 20 cm across. The mouth-arms and tentacles are a fused mass below the body with a few longer tentacles with frilly tips. It is a dirty brown-green in colour, the green colour coming from commensal algae growing on it. Not a vicious stinger.

Physalia physalis or Portuguese man-o-war. An elongated silver-blue float edged in magenta and purple, up to 30 cm long and 10 cm wide. It has a conspicuous transparent or light blue 'sail' held up by water pressure. Underneath the float is a community of different individuals: the Portuguese man-o-war is not one creature but many larval and adult forms somehow all working together as a single entity. Among its specialised organisms are some with very long stinging cells up to 30 metres long, capable of dealing painful and potentially very dangerous stings. These jellyfish should not be touched even when washed up on the beach and apparently dead.

There is no known antidote to jellyfish stings though there are a number of ways of obtaining relief. Dilute alkalis such as ammonium hydroxide, sodium bicarbonate or a freshly sliced onion applied to the wound have proved effective. Olive oil, sugar and ethyl alcohol or meths have been suggested. One tip which sounds promising is to use meat tenderiser, which apparently breaks down the protein base of the venom. If there are complications from a sting such as palpitations of the heart or breathlessness, medical help should be sought quickly.

When hauling up the anchor in an area infested with jellyfish be sure to wear gloves. The stinging tentacles, particularly of *Pelagia noctiluca* and the Portuguese man-o-war, often get caught up in anchor chain or rope and if you are pulling it up or flaking down with bare hands, you can easily be stung.

Sea urchins Take care not to get sea urchin spines in your feet when swimming or walking where they lie on the bottom. Some sea urchins have a mild venom, but the chief danger is from secondary infection when the spines break off in your feet. Wearing shoes is the best defence.

While sailing across the sea you are closer to the water and more aware of things in and on it.

8
Mediterranean Pot-pourri

'The time has come', the Walrus said, 'To talk of many things: Of shoes and ships and sealing wax. Of cabbages and kings. Of why the sea is boiling hot. And whether pigs have wings.'

Lewis Carroll: *Through the Looking Glass*

This chapter contains an eclectic collection of information about the Mediterranean, on food and drink, yacht documentation, chartering, local customs, archaeological sites and useful books. Some of it is more concerned with travel on land, but all of it will be of interest to anyone who goes there.

Food

At first glance it might appear that there is no unifying factor in the cuisine and foods of different Mediterranean countries, but there is an underlying theme and that is climate. The classic definition of the Mediterranean climate, as the area between the northern limit of the olive tree and the northern limit of the palm grove, gives us the first element of this unity, the olive. The arid summers all but rule out pasture for cows and consequently their milk products. Butter, milk and cream rarely feature in the cuisine and are replaced by olive oil. Bread is used to mop up the olive oil from salads, meat and fish, and from the numerous other dishes covered liberally. Sauces using olive oil with tomato paste, onion, peppers, lemon, herbs and spices replace the butter and milk-based sauces found in northern countries. Yoghurt is used instead of cream, which is almost never found in sauces or desserts.

A second consequence resulting from the lack of pasture is the virtual absence of beef from the diet. In recent years cheap beef has been imported and substituted for the veal, goat and lamb which have been commonly used in Mediterranean dishes. The arid land cannot sustain mature cattle and so calves are eaten as veal. Sheep and goats can survive on the sparse vegetation that remains through the summer, and their milk is used instead of cows' milk to produce yoghurt and cheese, both of which last better in a hot climate than the milk itself.

As well as the olive, wheat and vines are cultivated all around the Mediterranean. It is hard to imagine how the desert sands in Libya and Tunisia once produced vast yields of wheat, but in the heyday of the Roman Empire what is now desert was the bread-basket of Italy. Today the wheat grown is not used exclusively for bread. The hard durum wheat

*paktos. The most perfect little
dieval harbour in Greece.*

115

for making pasta is cultivated extensively in the northern Mediterranean countries, and while the Italians are the pasta wizards of the world, many other countries also use pasta as a staple in their diet. Pastry ranges from the fancy creations of the French to the paper-thin *filo* pastry of the Greeks and Turks. *Filo* is wrapped around anything from cheese and spicy minced meat to nuts and raisins soaked in honey. Rice is also an important crop, used in the *paella* of Spain, *risotto* in Italy, and the *pilav* of Turkey and the Middle East.

These, then, are the essence of Mediterranean food. Olive oil replaces the dairy products used in northern Europe. Meat is basically veal, lamb and chicken. Seafood is prized, but costly. Bread, pastry, pasta and rice provide the staple carbohydrates. Seasonal vegetables – tomatoes, aubergines, green peppers, courgettes, cucumbers, carrots, lettuce, cabbage and the essential onion and garlic – provide the variety and colour found in the dishes. It all sounds rather basic compared to the dairy-based cuisine of the north, but as Arabella Boxer points out in her excellent *Mediterranean Cookbook*, the basic ingredients are combined in appealing and interesting ways and spiked with herbs and spices. 'Taken as a whole, the average diet of the Mediterranean countries, particularly in the east, is austere but supremely healthy. Based on grilled meat and fish, raw salads, bread, fruit, herbs and yoghurt, it provides a limited but to me very appealing diet. It would be hard to suffer a liver attack or a cardiac condition in a true Mediterranean area, for the animal fats consumed by the north Europeans and the Americans simply do not exist. The potential monotony of such a limited diet is offset by the use of herbs on the northern shores of the Mediterranean, and spices in the south.'

The different countries around the Mediterranean have different preferences for the herbs and spices most commonly used. In the North African countries spices predominate: coriander, cumin, caraway and saffron are used in Egypt and the countries of the Mahgreb, Tunisia, Algeria and Morocco. Chilli peppers are also extensively used and are most often encountered in *harissa*, a sauce made of tomato paste and hot chilli peppers. It is usually toned down for the tender palate unaccustomed to its normal fiery strength. In Spain the centuries of Arab rule significantly affected the cuisine and spices are the important additives flavouring Spanish food. *Paella* would be incomplete without saffron to give it its distinctive flavour.

In France and Italy, herbs are the important flavouring. In *bouillabaisse*, a dish Arabella Boxer describes as 'more truly typical of the Mediterranean than any other', parsley, thyme, fennel and the bay leaf are used. French cuisine utilises herbs and also spices in a rich and varied way for which it is justly famous. In Italy basil and oregano are the favourites. In Greece oregano is supreme, along with the lemon. With everything from a lamb chop to *avgolimoni* sauce, the acid juice of the lemon imparts a unique taste to the food. In Turkey, the Middle Eastern preference for certain herbs becomes evident with parsley the favourite, closely followed by chervil and dill. In the Middle East parsley and mint are used in everything from meat dishes to desserts.

Fish has traditionally been part of the Mediterranean diet and figures in the cuisine of all the countries around its shores. But lately it has become something of a luxury and prices, especially for shellfish and lobster, have rocketed. The reason has to do not so much with a depletion of fish stocks in the Mediterranean, but with the increased demand for fish by both local people and the increasing numbers of foreign tourists. This is a great shame as many countries, France and Italy especially, have novel and delicious fish dishes.

In recent years the exodus of sun-starved northerners to the shores of the Mediterranean has dented the traditional cuisine. In the popular tourist spots snack bars serve up hamburgers that taste like cardboard and miserly portions of cold chips. Pizza restaurants have sprung up from Gibraltar to Greece. And Coca-cola and Pepsi slug it out for the

onal vegetables provide the variety
colour found in Mediterranean
ne.

117

Open air markets provide the ingredients for simple picnic lunches in most of the Mediterranean countries. As well as fruit and vegetables there will be regional cheeses, cured meats and salamis, pick and the ubiquitous olive.

lion's share of the market from the Mahgreb to Syria. The traveller can ignore or embrace this food pollution according to his or her tastes. More insidious is the faking of food that is becoming more widespread as demand grows for expensive and popular dishes in a country. Food faking is easiest where rich sauces are used, such as in veal marsala and coq au vin, or in dishes where the main ingredient is mixed with other dominant ingredients such as lobster mornay and *bouillabaisse*. Pork and chicken can be used instead of the more expensive veal, monkfish instead of lobster, white fish for scampi, and a *bouillabaisse* made up from seafood leftovers. Most of such passing-off goes on in the restaurants of Spain, France and Italy, and tends to occur in the richer and more complicated dishes. Plainer fare is more difficult and less profitable to fake.

...ou can sit down to a meal . . . .

Wine

The Greeks and the Romans were both fond of a good tipple. Odysseus on his travels pined for what he described as 'the best of all occasions' when the guests and feasters were assembled and 'the wine steward draws wine from the mixing bowl to pour into each cup in turn'. The Romans were famous for their excessive feasts washed down with copious quantities of wine. Their love of wine was such that wherever Roman rule spread viticulture quickly followed, providing wine to slake the thirst of foot soldier and general alike. In this way the vine spread from a few isolated parts of the Mediterranean across to the far boundaries of the Roman Empire.

119

Wine in the Mediterranean varies tremendously in quality from one country to another. The Cote du Rhone and Cote du Provence of France can be superb and reasonably priced wines. The *vin ordinaire* has probably been blended with wine from Sicily, though the French vehemently deny it. Italy produces excellent wines and gives the best value for money in the cheaper range. The *vino corriente* of Spain is eminently drinkable, but Spain produces excellent quality wines as well, not to mention the fine sherries of Jerez, its distinctive brandy and good liqueurs.

As you move farther east to Yugoslavia, Greece and Turkey the quality deteriorates. Yugoslavia produces some excellent white wines in the north, from Macedonia come some good reds, and in Turkey a few good reds can be found from the vineyards on the Aegean coast. But overall the quality and consistency cannot match the wines of France and Italy. You can drink a bottle of excellent wine, order another identical bottle and find it virtually undrinkable. The ingredients and the enthusiasm are there, but not the expertise to turn the grapes into consistently good wine.

In North Africa the wines of Tunisia, Algeria and Morocco vary immensely and again are not consistent. When the French administered this part of the world they planted extensive vineyards and produced some good wine. After the French departed the vineyards deteriorated and the expertise to turn the grapes into good wine was, alas, lost. Some quaffable wine at reasonable prices is bottled, but don't expect the variety and consistency of the products from the countries directly across the Mediterranean.

Individual and distinctive wines such as the *retsina* of Greece can be an acquired taste. Retsina is made by adding pine resin to the wine during fermentation, giving it a distinctive resiny flavour described by some as imparting a taste not dissimilar to certain brands of turpentine; others consider it a unique tangy wine. You either like it or hate it. The ancient Greeks appear to have liked it, or perhaps all wine then tasted of resin. In ancient amphorae and wine jugs traces of pine resin have been found, and it may have been used to seal the containers to prevent the wine going off, imparting the unique sappy taste. At the other end of the Mediterranean, the blended wines of the Jerez region in Spain are known world-wide. The various sherries — more than just the familiar dry pale *fino*, dark nutty *amontillado*, and the sweeter *oloroso* and cream sherry — are produced from subtle blends of wines of different types and ages. They are made on the *solera* system, where some of the oldest wine is mixed with the next oldest and so on down to the new, so that the newest wine absorbs some of the flavour and character of the older ones.

In the oldest wine producing area in the world, you will have no difficulty finding wine of some description. There are few countries around the Mediterranean that don't produce large quantities of wine for their own consumption and some of it is excellent; and whatever its merits or demerits, it is all comparatively cheap.

Cheers, Sante, Yammas, Sharife, Salute.

Flora

Over the 8000 years that man cleared and cultivated the land around the Mediterranean, it has been extensively modified. His animals have over-grazed, land was cleared by simply burning off all the vegetation, forests were felled to build fleets of ships, and trees of all kinds were cut for fuel for cooking and small industries like ore smelting and firing pottery. The ancient writers described lush green and fertile islands that are now arid and support little more than the stunted plants of *macquis* and *garrigue*. Medieval writers described great forests populated by boar, wolves and bears; long ago they were driven out and the forests cut down so that not a trace remains. What is now desert in North

Wine is still made in the traditional way in many of the smaller villages around the Mediterranean — here on Levkas in Greece.

The rock-rose, Cistus albidus. From its Corsican name, macchia, we get the generic term macquis.

Africa was a great grain-growing region. Even plants we think of as quintessentially Mediterranean turn out to be introduced species, among them the palms, loquat, oranges and lemons, bouganvillea, jasmine, cacti and quite possibly the olive. The clearing of the coniferous forests on the shores and the subsequent introduction of sheep and goats, which nibble away any new growth, radically altered the landscape. Most of the forested areas were turned into one of the two related types of vegetation that are common to this day.

Macquis is the thick, tangled vegetation typically growing on coastal regions, although it can extend a considerable distance inland. It is a mixture of low bushes and shrubs growing 2 to 4 metres high, that have adapted to survive in their exposed and windy situation. A considerable number of species are represented, including broom (*Genista cinera*), tree heather (*Erica arborea*), strawberry tree (*Arbutus unedo*), myrtle

(*Myrtus communis*), kermes oak (*Quercus coccifera*) and the rock-rose (*Cistus albidus*). The latter is interesting since its Corsican name is *macchia* and it is probably a corruption of this that gave *macquis* its name. The aromatic herbs and the plants of the *macquis* give off a distinctive aroma and with an offshore wind you can often smell it several miles out to sea. Napoleon said of his native Corsica that he could recognise the island with his eyes shut, by the smell of the rock-rose alone.

These plants have adapted to their exposed habitat in a variety of ways. Because there are no tall trees to stop the wind or to shade the plants, and water is scarce in summer, the biggest danger for the plants of the *macquis* is water loss. To prevent this plants like myrtle and the rock-rose secrete an oily or gummy substance over their leaves. The leaves of broom and buckthorn are very small so that the least surface area possible is presented. The plants must all be sturdy with good roots to withstand the buffeting of the wind, and the stems and branches tend to be dense and knotty. The wood of tree heather is so dense that it will not burn and is used for the bowls of pipes.

Garrigue grows on land where even the tenacious *macquis* cannot survive. Generally the plants are less than half a metre in height and flower briefly in the spring before the hot summer sun withers them to dry brown stems and leaves. Many common culinary herbs are found in *garrigue*: thyme, sage, rosemary, hyssop and rue. Their different flavours largely come from the aromatic oils they secrete to prevent water loss. Like *macquis*, the plants are adapted to conserve water. Some disappear underground during the summer and spend the hot dry period as bulbs in the cooler earth. The sea quill (*Urginea maritima*) exists as a large bulb in the summer, but with the first autumn rain it grows at an astonishing rate and then flowers.

In the spring the *garrigue* is transformed: many of the plants have vividly coloured flowers. Fields of red poppies have patches of other wildflowers: yellow irises, orange and yellow crocuses, white narcissus, and the delicate green and purple fritillary. Orchids are well represented, many of them of exquisite shape and colour. In some areas such as Crete, there are a large number of native orchids.

In many of the countries around the Mediterranean reafforestation has been underway for some time. Nearly all of the new pine forests are composed of Douglas fir, which grows quickly and easily. Although the planting has been undertaken for good reasons, to stop soil erosion and to provide wood for building and paper pulp, pine forests are not hospitable habitats. The dense needles prevent light getting to the ground so few plants can survive there, and the resin and dead needles decompose in the soil to form acids which prevent plants growing in it.

In a few parts of the Mediterranean, in inaccessible and relatively unpopulated areas, forest and vegetation remains that is still much like that of 2000 years ago. The holm oak (*Quercus ilex*) and cork oak (*Quercus suber*) cover parts of the coasts of Sardinia and Spain. Aleppo pines (*Pinus halepensis*) and cypress grow in parts of Macedonia and the Greek islands. It is difficult to imagine most of the Mediterranean coast covered in thick deciduous forest and undergrowth, and populated by wild boar, wolves and bears. But so it was, and we can only hope that what remains is protected for the future.

Bureaucracy and Documentation

In the Mediterranean all yachts are subject to considerable paperwork. Part of it is to do with people departing from one country and arriving in another, and the immigration authorities and the police want to keep tabs on this. However, the greater part is to do with Customs. You are chugging around in an expensive bit of machinery crammed full of other expensive items such as radios, electronic equipment, cameras, liferaft, dinghy and outboard, and the Customs want to make sure you are not importing anything without paying the appropriate import and other taxes for their country. They also want to make sure you are not smuggling illegal substances, weapons or aliens into the country. The amount of red tape, documentation and officials one has to deal with to sail a yacht around seems to bug some yachtsmen. In some countries one has to deal with a couple of different officials and fill in several forms just in moving from one harbour to another within the country. To yachtsman unaccustomed to this, it all appears to be an unnecessary impediment to what was an attempt to get away from a regulated existence, bureaucracy and officialdom very much included.

There is no universal panacea that will cut through all this red tape. You must submit to it and be processed. If you try to hurry things along, throw a tantrum, pull rank or drop names, the process will inevitably and inexplicably take longer. Better to understand that these officials are underpaid beings caught in a bureaucratic web that is not of their making, and if they do not do their job then someone higher up will ask questions. You will come across obnoxious little bureaucrats who make the process a great deal more tedious and prolonged than it need be, but most of the officials you deal with will not be of this ilk. Offering a bribe to speed things along is not recommended. In most of these countries it will simply offend the officials concerned, and in some places you will end up behind bars. In those others where a bribe may seem to facilitate the procedure, you establish a precedent for other people coming after you, or reinforce an undesirable habit which not everyone can afford. I have never bribed officials, but I do invite them aboard for coffee, a whisky, a cigarette and a chat. Although some have asked for whisky or cigarettes in larger quantities, they do not seem to be offended if you don't give them a 'gift'. The conviviality and a drink have sufficed.

The Siesta

In the summer afternoons when temperatures are at their highest, local people retreat into their homes or cafés and stay there until the cool of early evening. As Noel Coward observed of another continent, 'only mad dogs and Englishmen go out in the midday sun'. Even the commercial practices of the EEC countries, formulated in colder northerly climes, have not dented the custom of stopping work in the afternoon. For those used to a nine-to-five working day it takes a little while to adjust to the fact that one is not going to be able to see anyone or buy anything in the siesta period. Its exact timing varies from country to country and often locally as well. Generally, between 1400 and 1800 local time shops and offices close; many will be open for business only in the morning and do not reopen in the afternoon or evening. In some countries grocers, bakers, butchers and fruit and vegetable shops do not open again in the evening, so you must buy all your provisions in the morning.

In the case of hospitals, pharmacies, doctors, dentists and some essential services, a roster system operates for the siesta period and the evening. Officials such as Customs, port police, marina staff and harbourmasters all take a siesta. If you are clearing from a

...metimes your papers will be checked by a patrol boat, as here in Turkey.

harbour or country and must get papers processed, remember to start in time so it can be completed before the siesta begins. When clearing a country you will often have to visit several offices which may be some distance apart, so it is a matter of getting to them all as well as getting the paperwork done before siesta.

Instead of getting frustrated because you cannot get things done, do as the locals do and take a siesta yourself. Not only will you avoid the hottest part of the day, but you will be fresh for the evening. In most Mediterranean countries the evening meal is eaten late and without a siesta you may find yourself nodding off.

125

There are not only ancient remains from the Greeks and Romans, but many fine Medieval castles and buildings as well.

Archaeological and Historical Sites

A sad tale was told in a recent holiday brochure. On a yachting holiday, a charterer stumbled across a superb Roman mosaic floor on a small island off the Turkish coast. The charterers kept the discovery to themselves until they were able to tell. the proper authorities about it. Somehow the news leaked out, and by the time the authorities got there the whole mosaic floor had been roughly removed, probably destroying part of it in the process.

The desire to possess a piece of the ancient world exists in most of us. Why we need an ancient coin, pottery shards, part of a mosaic, a vase or oil lamp, a scarab or some other relic is difficult to understand when most of us have only a scant knowledge of the ancient world. Why are we not satisfied with copies that even experts cannot always distinguish from originals? I have no explanation for this greed, at least no brief answers. What is more important is the vandalising of sites that occurs in the search for souvenirs from the

Venetian fort at Astros in Greece.

ancient world. Such vandalism makes the work of the archaeologists nearly impossible. Just moving ancient bric-a-brac around a site makes it a hundred-fold more difficult to piece together a picture of life in those times. If unique pieces are removed, all of us are deprived of ancient works of art when they are finally housed in some private collection and not in a public museum.

All one can do is to make a plea to yachtsmen not to vandalise these sites, especially since many of them, particularly in Greece and Turkey, are accessible only by sea. The yachtsman has a special duty to refrain from nibbling away at the bits of the ancient world still remaining and to educate his fellow users of the sea to do the same.

There are many ancient sites around the Mediterranean. A few are familiar by name to almost everyone: Pompeii, Delphi, the Parthenon in Athens, Ephesus, the Pyramids, and the Valley of the Kings at Luxor. These well known places make up a small fraction of the total number. The ancients were great colonisers as well as great builders and the Mediterranean was a busy sea crossed by merchant and naval fleets. According to Willard Bascom's *Deep Water, Ancient Ships,* 'Between 750 and 550 BC the Greeks founded some 250 colony-cities, most of which were seaport towns around the Mediterranean and Black seas and some of which have been continuously inhabited ever since. The city-state of Corinth founded Syracuse on Sicily; Miletus established Sinope and Trapezus on the Black Sea and Sybaris in the arch of the Italian boot; Megara set up Byzantium in the Turkish straits; and Sparta established Tarentum at the tip of the heel of Italy.' From Spain to Asia Minor, from Morocco across the sea to Syria, there are literally hundreds of ancient sites, many of them virtually unknown outside archaeological circles and some unexcavated. In most of their countries the finds made are displayed in museums, with models of the site to give an idea of what it originally looked like. Unfortunately the best exhibits are usually in the capital city, but there is an increasing trend to build small local museums on a site to display finds made there, or in a regional centre.

In a boat, one is in the enviable position of being able to approach an ancient site and see it as a seaman might have several thousand years ago. Often the approach from the sea is the most attractive one, as it so often is for contemporary villages and towns, and in some places you still berth in the ancient harbour. Even if you have little interest in what has been left behind since the Greeks and Romans, few are unimpressed by the brilliant engineering feats carried out, and only the hard-hearted can deny the romance of anchoring in a deserted bay close by the ruins of a theatre on the shore.

Apart from the cities, towns, temples and tombs of antiquity, there are numerous monuments to the civilisations that followed: the churches and murals of Byzantium; the Norman cathedrals and churches and especially the fusion of Arab and Norman architecture in Sicily. The massive castles of the Knights of St John in Rhodes and Malta. The opulent palaces and the castles along the trade routes of the Venetians and Genoese. The softer rounded Moorish architecture in Spain. The massive fortifications of the Crusaders, with Krak de Chevaliers in Syria towering over them all. The pencil-thin minarets of Ottoman mosques and the opulence and indulgence of Topkapi Palace in Istanbul. The solid Romanesque and the Gothic reaction to it of the Christian world. The Baroque and neo-Gothic revival. The eccentric architecture of Gaudi in Barcelona. The Mediterranean is a treasure trove of man's attempts to raise stone, brick and mortar to leave enduring monuments to ideas and beliefs, and to keep the unbelievers out.

In the 18th century Samuel Johnson was able to state: 'The grand object of travelling is to see the shores of the Mediterranean. On these shores were the four great empires of the world – the Assyrian, the Persian, the Greek and the Roman. All our religion, almost all our arts, almost all that sets us above savages, has come to us from the shores of the

e Temple to Athena at Heracleia-der-Latmos in Turkey. Fine ashlar sonry still in perfect condition more n two thousand years after it was lt.

Mediterranean.' We can add to that list of empires, starting with the civilised court of Byzantium and progressing through the Renaissance to the legacy of the Papacy in the West and the last glimmer of the Ottoman empire in the East. Monuments from all the ages of man abound on the shores of the Mediterranean, and for those to whom sailing also means getting to interesting places – this is the place.

Carved theatrical masks from the theatre at Myra in Turkey.

Guide-books

Yachting pilot books and guides often contain a large amount of information unrelated to finding and getting into harbours or anchorages: information about the history and customs of a place, about its character and 'feel', the local industry and agriculture, cuisine, the sort of things that might attract one there in preference to another place or that might be interesting anyway. If such books don't, they should; however any such peripheral information must be squeezed in with the essential navigation and pilotage data, and some tend to reflect the authors' tastes. Most of us want a more detailed account of a country or place. Guide-books offering such information exist for all of the Mediterranean countries, but like all books some are to be savoured while some are just plain bad at the job they purport to do.

For historical and archaeological information the *Blue Guides* published by A and C Black are the doyen of them all. They are crammed with information and are about as up to date and accurate as you will get on such matters without going to academic tomes. Some people find them a bit formal and hard going, but at least the information is there in detail and authority, features which are lamentably lacking in many other guides. *Blue Guides* are available in hard cover and paperback and currently cover Spain, Northern Italy, Rome, Sicily, Venice, Malta, Greece, Athens, Crete, Istanbul and Cyprus. More readable but still well informed in a more chatty style, are the Collins' *Companion Guides.* These books are written by experts on the various countries and currently cover the south of Spain, southwest France, the south of France, Tuscany, Rome, Southern Italy, Venice, Yugoslavia, the Greek islands, southern Greece, mainland Greece and Turkey. Descending to rough and tough guides, there are the Routledge & Kegan Paul *Rough Guides* to Spain, France, Tuscany and Umbria, Yugoslavia, Greece, Israel, Tunisia and Morocco. These not only cover some less popular regions, but cater for unorthodox travel, and people on their own with limited finances and a desire to get beyond the usual tourist spots.

Apart from these series of books, there are often one-off guides that provide some of the best information on a particular country and its people. For these you will have to do a little research, but the sort of books I am thinking of are Patrick Leigh Fermor's books on Greece, Lord Kinross on Turkey, and Norman Lewis on Italy. These are not guide-books as such, but they often give an insight into a country and its culture that the guide-book cannot. As well as writers in this century, it can be interesting to read classic accounts by 19th century travellers in the Mediterranean. Many of these are being reissued, and apart from describing a place as it was a hundred or so years ago, a lot of these books are amusing and erudite and still a pleasure to read. Foremost among these is Kinglake's *Eothen,* Curzon's *Visit to the Monasteries in the Levant,* and Morritt's *A Grand Tour.*

There are a number of classic accounts of sailing in the Mediterranean. Ernle Bradford cruised around after the Second World War and wrote a number of books including *Ulysses Found,* an account of the geographical places that can still be identified as those described in Homer. Immediately after the war George Millar sailed through the French canals and on to Greece, and in *Isabel and the Sea* he describes the terrible damage inflicted on the Mediterranean countries during the war. More recently Tim Severin constructed a replica of a Homeric scouting galley and retraced the path of Jason and the Argonauts in search of the golden fleece and recently the voyage of Ulysses on his way home from the Trojan War.

In the end, the sort of guide-books you get will reflect your interests and the amount of time you are going to stay in a country. 'The only useful guide-book', Aldous Huxley was fond of saying, 'will be the one which he himself has written', but given that few of us have the ability or the inclination to do this, we must be content with criticising those that already exist. The longer you are in a country and the more interested you become in it, inevitably the more books you will accumulate on its different facets. One of the enduring problems I have on my boat is finding room for all the books I like to have around me, old friends and new finds; and the more familiar one becomes with all the sources of inform-ation on a place the easier it is to flip through a new guide-book and dismiss it or avidly pull out your wallet to buy a copy.

Chartering Holidays

Deciding on what type of sailing holiday to take depends on all sorts of factors, not the least being the size of your wallet, your experience, your inclinations and those of your crew or family. If you are taking an all-singing-and-dancing luxury skippered charter, then it simply boils down to where and with whom, so here I will concentrate on the more usual choice between flotilla and bareboat charter.

Most flotilla companies require only that you know how to sail a dinghy or a small cruiser, and that you are accompanied by someone to assist you in crewing the boat. In some areas where the conditions are more demanding and the passages longer, the company may require that you have more experience. A bareboat charter company will generally want some sort of certificate attesting to your ability or a recommendation from a recognised yacht club.

That is the bare minimum required, but you should think seriously about preparing yourself for a flotilla or bareboat holiday before blithely signing the cheque. A reputable charter company worried about your experience, or rather the lack of it, will advise you to take a 'learning to sail' course either in your own country or in the Mediterranean. The latter means you get a holiday in the sun and also get on the water and learn to sail in a competent way. Many of the companies, or associated companies, offer 'learning to sail' or refresher courses directly tailored to the holiday you are going on. Don't take umbrage if a company suggests you should take one of these courses: a weekend learning course before your holiday will enable you to enjoy it from the start with little of the confusion and panic that often accompanies the first few days.

When you are weighing up the pros and cons of whether to go on a flotilla or bareboat, be wary of choosing the option on the edge of your experience. In many cases it would be better to choose a flotilla over the bareboat option, even though you are eminently qualified to take out a bareboat. In any case most flotillas offer enough freedom for you to do your own thing. What often happens on a sailing holiday is that plans are made to cover too much ground, visit too many places and get in as much sea time as possible. There seems little point in visiting another country to spend so much time away from it, out at sea. Even worse, it is likely that the crew, whether family or not, will probably mutiny at some point because they want more time ashore and a chance to enjoy new places. Strict timetables leave little room to manoeuvre should the weather make it difficult to get a bareboat back to the charter base, and remember that if you do not, it will cost you money. Flexibility and not too much ambition in the timetable will let all concerned enjoy both the sailing and the time ashore and will not push your ex-perience to the limits.

Even experienced skippers with their own boats should remember that they will be on a strange boat with different handling characteristics and different gear from their own. You will be sailing in an area where the weather can change abruptly without warning, and the sea go from a millpond to wave-tossed in no time at all. Those who have sailed there know that the Mediterranean is not always the blue sea ruffled by zephyrs that the brochures so often depict. It has a malevolence as well.

Families or singles

When choosing a holiday, look carefully over the brochures to see if the company is aiming at families or singles. With a bareboat holiday this is obviously not important since you can tailor the holiday to your group. But for shore-based and flotilla holidays the style and content of the brochure will suggest whether you will be the only family in a group of singles, or vice versa. Some brochures aim unashamedly at singles and couples unencumbered with children, whereas others provide additional family facilities such as a nanny to look after the children so you can get away to do some sailing.

Most flotilla holidays happily accommodate families, and in the summer holiday break the majority of boats will have children on board. It's a good holiday for all concerned with plenty to do on the boat and ashore, for both parents and children. Remember that on a bareboat holiday there will not be other children around for your offspring to play with, whereas on a flotilla there will be and this keeps them out of your hair. On a skippered charter, check first to see if children the age of yours will really be welcome, and if there will be enough for them to occupy themselves with. It may be that all that leisure you are seeking will not appeal as much to young children.

Costs and when to go

For nearly all charters the cost varies with the time of the year. High season is June, July and August and always the most expensive: it is the hottest and sunniest time of the year, the sea has warmed up, and for families with school-age children it is the only time available. For some areas, in particular the Aegean, the settled summer conditions bring the strongest winds, strong enough that flotillas change their itinerary and bareboats are kept in harbour, so choose your area with care to avoid the windy spots in the high season.

Early season runs from April or May to early June. There may be some rain and unsettled weather but not enough to ruin your holiday. The days are warm and the nights pleasantly cool, the only snag being that the sea is still cold. On the whole, though, it is my favourite time of year, when the Mediterranean is clothed in an uncharacteristic green and a profusion of vividly coloured wildflowers.

Late season runs from September to October. Again there may be some rain and unsettled weather, but mostly the days are warm and the nights mild. The advantage of late season over early is that the sea is at its warmest. Late season is often more popular than early for the simple reason that a bad summer in Europe precipitates a scramble for any late slots so that some sort of holiday can be salvaged.

While scanning the brochures think about early and late season holidays, where considerable savings can be made. Moreover you will see a different Mediterranean from the sun-baked one depicted by the brochures – and not an unpleasing place at that.

When adding up the likely cost of a holiday, keep an eye on the hidden costs that must be worked into the final figure. First, the additional charges that can be made if flights and transfers are included in the price; fuel surcharges should the price of aviation fuel increase; currency surcharges should the exchange rates fluctuate after the brochure is printed; airport taxes, which may be added to the price although they are normally costed into the overall price; travel insurance; and the cost of the transfer from the airport if this is

Flotillas are more sailing-in-company than follow-the-leader and most flotillas allow a substantial amount of independent sailing.

not included in the overall price. Second, there are the additional charges arising during the holiday: some companies charge a small non-refundable security deposit although normally you will deposit a cheque for this; charges for the paperwork for clearing out from the base harbour; the cost of diesel and cooking gas used; charges for any additional equipment you may want such as a sailboard, outboard motor, cruising chute or spinnaker; and dues that will be paid in harbours en route. Add all of these additional costs into the overall package price and you are looking at a substantial increase. It may be that an all-in price which initially appears high, works out in fact to be cheaper than a lower price with all the extra costs added on. One of the advantages of a flotilla is that many of the additional charges such as for paperwork, harbour dues, diesel and cooking gas, are included in the overall price. Bareboat prices, on the other hand, rarely include these costs.

Questions to ask the charter company

Concerning the boats and the charter operation, you need to ask the following questions. How old are the boats and what type are they? Are they all the same? If they are six or more years old they will have had a fair old hammering and may not be in the best condition.

What sort of winter maintenance is carried out? Is there a winter crew working on the boats all winter or is there a mad rush in the spring to do the refits? Does the season start with your charter?

When was the last major refit of the boats? For example, when did the engines last come out, to be stripped and inspected?

What age is the other equipment on the boats – the sails, dinghies, anchor chain, etc.?

What happens if there are breakages: who pays for what? What if a defect is serious enough to stop your sailing as much as you wanted to?

How many sailboards are provided on a flotilla and how old are they? Compute for yourself how much use one sailboard for a flotilla of twelve boats gets in one season. Can you hire a sailboard just for your own boat's use?

What other gear is provided, such as for snorkeling, cockpit cushions and a cockpit table for that all important *al fresco* life?

What charts and pilot books will be on your boat? What navigation equipment is there on board? This may not be all-important on flotilla, but it is on a bareboat charter where all too often the boats are ill-equipped for their task.

In most cases a boat advertised as sleeping six is comfortable for four, and a ten-berth boat is comfortable for six or seven. If an identical boat is at a boat show, have a realistic look at the berths and stowage arrangements. A family used to living together can often make use of all the available berths, but two couples, even if they are life-long friends will find the lack of privacy in a small boat difficult to cope with. Ironically, those thrown together in share-a-boat or pot-luck schemes seem to cope better with the crowded conditions.

Once you get satisfactory answers to these and any other questions, you have a firm base on which to select the company you will charter from. In the long run it pays to choose one of the longer standing companies who have been at the game for a while. Word of mouth from somebody who has chartered one of their boats before is usually the best recommendation. No brochure is going to tell you the whole truth about the boats or the charter area, and some will totally mislead you about both.

Equipping Yourself

Clothes Most people take too much and the wrong sort of clothing. Keep your clothing light and include at least two swimming costumes and several pairs of shorts and T-shirts: you'll be living in them most of the time. Take some light clothes, still casual, for that special meal ashore, but don't over-burden yourself with fancy dress or jackets as most of the time it is going to be too hot for it. When you set out from cooler northern climes wear several layers of easily discarded clothing so you can step out onto the shimmering tarmac looking a good deal cooler than you probably feel. Those with fair skins and freckles must remember to take a long-sleeved shirt and light trousers to keep the sun off arms and legs. A wide-brimmed hat or a visor such as favoured at Wimbledon is also a necessary piece of kit to keep the sun off the face. This is especially important for young children, who need a wide-brimmed hat that will not come off in a breeze rather than sun glasses. Pyjamas are effective for keeping the sun off in the day and you may need them at night in early and late season.

Don't forget a sturdy pair of shoes for the rough going up to a hilltop taverna, and a pair or two of trainers or canvas shoes that you don't mind getting wet: you need the latter for when sea urchins lurk just where you are going to clamber out of the dinghy, and as deck shoes.

In April, May and October pack some oilskins and a heavy wool jersey in case you meet some rough stuff. For the rest of the season a light waterproof anorak and a medium jersey and trousers will suffice unless you do some night passages on a bareboat charter – take away the sun and it can be surprisingly chilly with a bit of spray and wind in the wee hours of the morning. Add to this a heavy pair of gloves such as leather and canvas plumber's gloves and your wardrobe is complete. Pack it all into a sailing bag or similar that can be folded flat (where can you put a suitcase on a boat?) and check the time the flight leaves.

Navigator's kit On flotilla the basic equipment aboard the boat will enable you to get around safely, but to enhance your holiday it is not a bad idea to buy a chart of the area and a yachtsman's pilot to gen up on it. On the chart you can plot your course around the area, tidy it up afterwards and keep it as a memento of your holiday. The pilot will help you do some forward planning on the places you want to go to and the logical route taking the prevailing winds into account.

If bareboating, enquire whether there is a hand bearing compass on board and if not take your own. Similarly, if there are no good binoculars on board take a pair along: they may help you positively identify a harbour, a cape or wildlife as well as the mole on the young lady's shoulder in the boat anchored near you, and make following the coast more interesting for everyone. Pack a pair of Polaroid sunglasses as well for early visual identification of reefs and shoal water (see the chapter on navigation).

And don't forget your favourite pickles, sauces and spreads if you must have them. It can be difficult to find Picallili, mint sauce and Marmite along Turkey's Lycian coast. Coffee and tea may not be difficult to find but are worth taking as they can be expensive, two or three times what you would normally pay. And a jar of chemical milk for the odd times you won't be able to get tinned or long-life milk.

Your camera and enough film plus another roll. Most people run out and films can be difficult to find in some places. Moreover it is expensive and may be old stock.

A few paperbacks to read during any idle hours that might crop up. You can often exchange them for others.

A guidebook on the area or country you will be in adds interest to excursions ashore, and a cookbook tells you much about the national characteristics as well as about the local produce, fish and cuisine.

Potions and lotions to tan yourself and stop sunburn and windburn; add a chapstick for your lips. Mosquito repellent, and if you are especially vulnerable to mosquito bites, a cream to aid healing.

Pills or potions to counteract the inevitable traveller's diarrhoea that temporarily afflicts most of us on a brief visit to the Mediterranean, and pills to ward off seasickness until you find your sea legs. Obviously, any special medication, prescriptions etc.

A spare pair of spectacles in a hard case, or contact lenses: if you don't lose them in a stiff breeze during an accidental gybe you may lose them on the return trip from the barbecue. Also take the prescription.

Leave any valuable jewellery, especially non-waterproof watches, at home, and save the gucci shoes, leather handbag and suede jacket from saltwater stains by leaving them behind.

Passport, tickets and money.

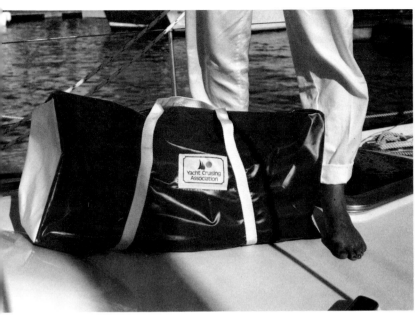

...ck everything into a sailing bag. Where are you going to put a suit-case on board?

Gazetteer of Charter Areas

Gibraltar Bareboat and skippered charter. From 'The Rock' you have access to Spain, Portugal and Morocco.

Spain Bareboat and skippered charter from various marinas along the coast and in the Balearic Islands (Majorca, Ibiza, Menorca). Although parts of Spain are crowded with considerable numbers of yachts, a little pre-planning and a natter with other yachtsmen will get you away from the crowds to some quite idyllic anchorages. Some companies offer a villa for a week and a week on a yacht.

France Mainly bareboat and skippered charter from various bases along the coast and in Corsica; semi-flotilla sailing from a base on the Cote d'Azur. In the south of France most of your sailing is between purpose-built marinas or harbours converted to marinas. There are few anchorages, and in the summer they will be far from deserted. *Corsica* is the better choice if you want deserted bays and majestic scenery. From there it is easy to get to Sardinia and the Tuscan islands including Elba.

Italy Bareboat and skippered charter from bases in northern and western Italy, Sardinia and from northern Italy in the Adriatic. Around the Ligurian coast most of the sailing is between marinas until you get down to the Tuscany coast and the Tuscan Islands. From Sardinia you have a superb if sometimes windy cruising area in the Straits of Bonifaccio and access to the rest of Sardinia and Corsica. From the northern Adriatic, most yachts head for Yugoslavia.

Malta Some bareboat and skippered charter. Most yachts head for Sicily and the Aeolian Islands using Malta more as a base than a cruising area.

Yugoslavia Flotilla, bareboat and skippered charter. The sheltered waters in between the many islands and the moderate summer winds make the area particularly suited to flotilla sailing; the fleets are concentrated between Sibenik and Dubrovnik and around Pula. For charterers who like deserted bays, the offshore islands and the much indented coast offer a wealth of choice. There are many attractive villages and fine old towns around the coast and on the larger islands, though there is not much in the way of shoreside entertainment.

Greece Shore-based, flotilla, bareboat and skippered charter. Flotilla sailing originated in Greece and it flourishes still. The many islands and the much indented coastline make up the best cruising areas in the Mediterranean, with a wide variety of scenery and a range of prevailing wind strengths in the summer. For beginners, the wind strengths are less in the Ionian and the Saronic Seas. In the Northern Sporades the winds are moderate, while in the Cyclades and the Dodecanese it is very windy in the summer when the *meltemi* is blowing. Bareboat charterers should steer clear of the Aegean east of longitude 23° E in the summer, particularly July and August, when the *meltemi* can blow at 30 to 40 knots on occasion. Outside of July and August wind strengths in the Aegean are considerably less.

Shore-based and learning-to-sail programmes are operated from a number of bases in the Ionian and the Saronic, where the wind strengths are more suited to dinghies and learner sailors. Villa–flotilla holidays with one week in a villa and one week sailing are also available in these areas.

Turkey Shore-based, flotilla, bareboat and skippered charter. Flotilla fleets and bareboats operate in the area between Kusadasi and Antalya, although most are concentrated between Bodrum and Fethiye. There are few islands but the broken and spectacular coastline makes up for this. In July and August when the *meltem* blows strongest, those protruding parts of the coast exposed to its full strength can be very windy even for the experienced yachtsman, but in the gulfs the wind strength is less and the sea flatter. The shore-based locations are generally windier than their Greek counterparts and more suitable for the advanced dinghy sailor and board sailor. Shoreside entertainment is cheap and plentiful.

Cyprus Shore-based and a few bareboats and skippered charters. Overall, there are not many places to sail to in Cyprus.

Tunisia A few bareboats and skippered charters.

Greece. Still one of the best cruising areas in the Mediterranean with a much indented coastline and islands scattered across the sea.

Appendix

Useful Books

BACKGROUND
The Mediterranean and the Mediterranean World in the Age of Phillip II vols I, II, Fernand Braudel. Fontana paperback. Don't be put off by the ponderous title: these two volumes are a mine of information on the geography, culture, economics and history of the Mediterranean.
Mankind and Mother Earth, Arnold Toynbee. Paladin p/b. Informative, readable history of the Mediterranean.
The Mediterranean, Richard Carrington. Weidenfeld & Nicholson.
The Prehistory of the Mediterranean, D.H. Trump. Pelican p/b.
On the Shores of the Mediterranean, Eric Newby. Harvill, also Picador p/b.
Ulysses Found, Ernle Bradford. Century Hutchinson p/b. Very readable, and written by a sailor.
The Jason Voyage, Tim Severin. Arrow p/b.
Mediterranean Cruising Handbook, Rod Heikell. Imray.
The Penguin Atlases of Ancient History/of Medieval History/of Modern History, Colin McEvedy. Penguin p/b. Three useful books to introduce you to the history of the Mediterranean.
The First Merchant Venturers, William Culican. Thames & Hudson.
Deep Water, Ancient Ships, Willard Bascom. David & Charles.

WEATHER
Heaven's Breath, Lyall Watson. Coronet p/b. Informative, amusing and erudite.
Cruising Weather, Alan Watts. Nautical.
This is Rough Weather Cruising, Erroll Bruce. Nautical.
Heavy Weather Sailing, Adlard Coles. Adlard Coles Ltd.
Meteorology at Sea, Ray Sanderson. Stanford Maritime.

HARBOURCRAFT AND ANCHORING
This is Boat Handling at Close Quarters, Dick Everit and Rodger Witt. Nautical.
Anchoring and Mooring Techniques Illustrated, Alan Grée. Adlard Coles Ltd.

NAVIGATION AND PILOTAGE
Practical Yacht Navigator, Kenneth Wilkes. Nautical.
Better Boat Handling, Des Sleightholme. Out of print, but good on piloting by eye, navigation, manoeuvring.
This is Fast Cruising, Peter Johnson. Nautical. Useful sections as well as much other general information.
The Coastal Cruising Handbook, Joseph Harand.
Electronics Afloat, Dag Pike. Nautical.

HEALTH
The Yachtsman's Doctor, Dr R.T. Counter. Nautical.
The Yachtsman's Emergency Handbook. Adlard Coles Ltd.

MARINE LIFE
The Natural History of the Mediterranean, Tegwyn Harris. Pelham. Useful guide to marine and shore life.

Hamlyn Guide to the Flora and Fauna of the Mediterranean Sea. Hamlyn p/b. Probably the best cheap reference book available.
Mediterranean Seafood, Alan Davidson. Penguin p/b. Contains useful line drawings and descriptions of many common species. And recipes!
Dangerous Marine Animals, Bruce Halstead, Cornell Maritime Press, USA.
Dangerous Animals of the Sea, Marc Ziliox. Ridge p/b.

MISCELLANEOUS
Mediterranean Cookbook, Arabella Boxer. Penguin p/b.
A Book of Mediterranean Food, Elizabeth David. Penguin p/b.
A Book of Middle Eastern Food, C. Rodon. Penguin p/b.
Food in History, Reay Tannahill. Paladin p/b.
Flowers of the Mediterranean, Anthony Huxley and Oleg Polunin.

CRUISING GUIDES AND INFORMATION
Reed's Mediterranean Almanac. Published annually, early each year.
Mediterranean Cruising Handbook, Rod Heikell. Imray, 1988 (2nd Ed.).
East Spain Pilot, Robin Brandon. Imray.
Guida Nautica Turistica y Deportiva de Espana: Capitanes de Yates. In Spanish, with plans.
South France Pilot, Robin Brandon. Imray.
Annuaire de Nautisme. Les Editions de Chabassol. Annual directory in French.
Votre Livre du Bord, Bloc Marine. Annual directory with plans and photographs in French.
Cruising French Waterways, Hugh McKnight. Stanford Maritime. Very thorough and also readable: the best book on the canals and rivers.
Italian Waters Pilot, Rod Heikell. Imray.
The Tyrrhenian Sea, H.M. Denham. John Murray.
Porticcioli d'Italia, Bruno Ziravello. In Italian.
156 Porti d'Italia. Instituto Geografico de Agostini. In Italian, with harbour plans and photos.
Adriatic Pilot, T. and D. Thompson. Imray. The Yugoslavian coast.
The Adriatic, H.M. Denham. John Murray.
Greek Waters Pilot, Rod Heikell. Imray.
The Aegean, H.M. Denham. John Murray.
The Ionian to the Anatolian Coast, H.M. Denham. John Murray.
Turkish Waters Pilot, Rod Heikell. Imray.
Pocket Guide to the Southeast Aegean, Rod Heikell and Mike Harper. Imray.
Turkey and the Dodecanese Cruising Pilot, Robin Petherbridge. Adlard Coles Ltd.
A Bridge and Galley Guide to Tunisia, Ann Maurice and Bryan Lockyear. McMillan Graham.

National Tourist Offices in London

Gibraltar Tourist Office, 4 Arundel Great Court, Strand, London WC2
Spanish National Tourist Office, 57 St James St, London SW1
French Tourist Office, 178 Piccadilly, London W1
Italian State Tourist Office, 1 Princes St, London W1
Maltese Tourist Office, 16 Kensington Square, London W8
Yugoslav National Tourist Office, 143 Regent St, London W1
Greek National Tourist Organisation, 195–7 Règent St, London W1
Turkish Tourism Information Office, Egypt House, 168 Piccadilly, London W1

(South) Cyprus High Commission, 211 Regent St, London W1
Israel Government Tourist Office, 18 Great Marlborough St, London W1
Egyptian Tourist Office, Egypt House, 168 Piccadilly, London W1
Tunisian National Tourist Office, 7a Stafford St, London W1
Algerian Consulate, 54 Holland Park, London W11
Moroccan Tourist Office, 174 Regent St, London W1

Other Useful Addresses
Cruising Association, Ivory House, St Katharine Dock, London E1 9AT
Royal Yachting Association, RYA House, Romsey Rd., Eastleigh, Hants.
Little Ship Club, at The Naval Club, 38 Hill St. London, W1X 8DP

Index

Adriatic Sea 17
Aegean Sea 18, 19, 21
Albania 18
Algeria 20, 32
Alps 23
anabatic wind 27
anchor 39, 41, 43, 49, 55, 76
  defensive 64
  dragging 48, 64, 66, 67, 69, 76
  fore & aft 64
  fouled 50, 56, 64, 67, 76
  in tandem 65
  light 69
  raising 67
  roller 48
  second 65, 66, 69
  signal 69
  stern 46
  third 65
  watch 67, 69
  weigh 67
  winch 59, 67, 68
angina 88
anti-fouling paint 106
anticyclone 23

Arab 129
archaeological site 127, 129
arifi 32
Atlantic Ocean 22
Azores 22, 23

babies 92
Balearics 16
Balkans 23
bareboat, charter 132
battery 82
bearing 67, 72
  clearing 72
  transit 72, 73
berthing lines 52
binoculars 75
bise 32
boathook 51, 53
boomkin 48
bora 24, 27, 32, 36
borasco 32
borini 32
bottom, sea 55
bouillabaisse 110, 117
bow roller 47, 59

bows-to mooring 39, 42, 46, 48, 49, 64
bowsprit 48
Braudel, Ferdinand 22
breakwater 51
Bruce, anchor 48, 57
buffer zone 27
buoyed lines 53, 67
bouys 70
bura 32
Byzantium 14, 129

CQR anchor 48, 55, 56
Camargue 102
carbine clip 52
Coriolis effect 27
chafe 52, 59
chain, anchor 41, 43, 57, 68
chain necklace, anchor, 67
chart 60, 70, 76, 82
charter 43, 132, 135
cheese 115
chergui 28, 32
children 89, 92
chili 28, 32
cholera 87